DATE DUE

MY 6 '02			
MY 28 '02			
OC 7 '03			

DEMCO 38-296

HOME BUSINESS MADE EASY

A Step-by-Step Road Map to Selecting and Starting a Home Business That Fits Your Interests, Lifestyle, and Finances

BY DAVID HANANIA

OASIS PRESS

The Oasis Press®/ PSI Research
Grants Pass, Oregon

Published by The Oasis Press®
© 1992, 1998 by David Hanania

This publication is designed to provide accurate and authoritative information in regard
to the subject matter covered. It is sold with the understanding that the publisher is not
engaged in rendering legal, accounting, or other professional service. If legal advice or
other expert assistance is required, the services of a competent professional person
should be sought.

> *— from a declaration of principles jointly adopted by a committee of*
> *the American Bar Association and a committee of publishers.*

Please direct any comments, questions, or suggestions regarding this book to
The Oasis Press®/PSI Research: Editorial Department
P.O. Box 3727
Central Point, OR 97502
(541) 479-9464 *telephone*
(541) 476-1479 *fax*
info@psi-research.com *email*

The Oasis Press® is a Registered Trademark of Publishing Services, Inc., an
Oregon corporation doing business as PSI Research.

Hanania, David, date.
   Home business made easy: a step-by-step road map to selecting and
starting a home business that fits your interests, lifestyle, and
finances / by David Hanania. — 2nd ed.
     p.   cm. — (PSI successful business library)
Includes bibliographical references and index.
ISBN 1-55571-428-5
   1. Home-based businesses. I. Title. II. Series.
HD2333.H37 1998
658'.041 — DC21
                                     97-40114

Printed in the United States of America
Second edition 10 9 8 7 6 5 4 3 2 1 0

 Printed on recycled paper when available.

Table of Contents

To Phyllis

my wife, my love,

my friend

Acknowledgments

In writing this book, I have drawn on many business and personal relationships and experiences. To those people in my long career who have contributed to my personal business success, my thanks.

More specifically, my appreciation to Dr. William Kleiber, a leading career consultant and psychotherapist, for his contributions to Chapter 2; and to Mark Director, an outstanding attorney, for his contributions to Chapter 6. For Michael D. Jenkins, CPA and attorney, for his input on additions to Chapter 6. For Bill Alexander's accounting contributions, Pat Casey's long hours in editing and interviewing, and Diane Averill's added touches, my gratitude.

I particularly want to acknowledge Vickie Reierson, C.C. Dickinson, Francie Marks, and Melody Joachims for their help in organizing and designing this book.

Finally, Joanne Bartoli helps me make things happen. She has been my right hand for over 14 years and any words fall far short in expressing my deep gratitude.

Standing alone, my special thanks to my wife Phyllis, whose encouragement and patience were an inspiration in writing this book.

About the Author

From starting his first entrepreneurial enterprise at age 11, to opening his first restaurant at 19, launching a mail-order company in his twenties, through founding, buying, building and selling over 30 businesses in 5 diverse industries, to launching his most recent venture at an age when most people think of retiring, David Hanania continuously proves that he thrives on the challenge of creating successful businesses.

While CEO of a publicly-held company, Mr. Hanania was appointed United Nations Day Chairman by President Ford, and received the International Amity Award from President Carter's Friendship Force for his leadership in promoting international goodwill.

The author has been directly involved in product design and engineering, financing, marketing, sales, and strategic planning, as well as industrial, stockholder and government relations. He personally developed several patents which are widely used to improve equipment safety.

Mr. Hanania is recognized as a pioneer in manufactured housing, as he was instrumental in leading the industry into many breakthroughs in marketing and design.

Not one to confine himself to one field, the author has founded businesses in a variety of industries, including construction, real estate development, housing, publishing, mail order, and restaurants. One company he started from home for less than five hundred dollars and later sold is now earning a profit of over five hundred thousand dollars per year for its current owners.

The author has served on the boards of many corporations, as well as Ithaca College's Business School. His wealth of experience makes him a popular lecturer, and he is frequently interviewed on television, radio, and by newspapers and magazines as an expert on home business and entrepreneurship.

He built a successful public multidivisional company employing over 5,000 people in eight states. This diverse company produced mobile homes, garden tractors, manufactured housing, and school furniture, as well as leisure, holiday, defense, and industrial products. He sold his stock interest, and retired as CEO, but after a couple of months he was launching his next new idea.

David Hanania then founded the Home Business Institute to give a broad range of people access to the entrepreneurial expertise he had accumulated in his varied adventures in businesses. The Home Business Institute is the leading national membership organization bringing information, services, literature, and benefits to its members.

While building businesses by day, Mr Hanania also managed to fit in getting two college degrees at night. He received his Bachelor of Business Administration from City College of New York, and his Master's in Industrial Management from New York University. He resides in White Plains, New York.

Preface

A great number of people want or need to make extra money. Many of these people are contemplating "doing something from home." For some, if they could start a business part time at home while being employed elsewhere so much the better, and so much the safer. Others are unemployed, or dissatisfied with their current employment, and want to be able to support themselves by working at home. Still others are fed up with commuting, want to be at home with their children, are bored with retirement, or simply want to be their own boss.

Add all these up and you have a huge number of people looking to break into the home-based business field. Where do these people go for information and answers to questions such as: What business is right for me? And, how do I get started?

Some of my friends and business acquaintances fall into the groups I have just described — even my wife and my secretary wanted to start home businesses. Having started businesses (some from home) and headed companies myself, it was natural that they came to me for advice. I tried and hopefully succeeded in helping these people clarify their thinking and direction as they selected, started, and operated their businesses.

Their questions led me to start checking the available literature about home-based businesses. I found some interesting books with information that was useful, but I also found a very profound gap. As I saw it, there was nothing available to the person contemplating a home business on how to select the right one. Also, much of the literature focused on many peripheral issues that were relatively unimportant to the home business entrepreneur. As a result, I felt the readers could not readily extract the important from the unimportant. In this maze it would be difficult, and possibly even costly, for the fledgling entrepreneur to logically follow the important steps he or she should address in forming and operating a home business. Hence the start of this book.

As one thing led to another, I found myself deeply involved in writing a book, not only to address the void in the selection process, but also to direct the reader in simple, concise language to the important points one should address in starting a business.

My paramount goal was to develop a guide that the reader could easily follow to go from the idea of wanting a home-based business to the reality of selecting it, starting it, operating it, and finally making it grow. Ultimately, this led to a simple step-by-step road format to guide the reader through this process.

In writing *Home Business Made Easy*, I have taken the roles of guide, teacher, counselor, advocate, and friendly business advisor. I have enjoyed most the role of friendly business advisor trying his best to guide you in your quest for a satisfying business.

Read on friend — I do hope this book will help you select, start, and build a very satisfying and successful business from home.

David Hanania

Introduction

Did you know that just by purchasing this book, you may be taking part in one of the fastest growing trends in America today — that of the home-based business? *The Wall Street Journal* says that by the year 2000, over 35 million people will work from their homes either full-time, part-time, or in their spare time. Look at how this figure has grown over the past several years. In 1985, the U.S. Bureau of Labor Statistics said more than 8 million Americans worked a substantial number of hours from their homes; by 1988, that number was 13 million; by the end of 1991 it grew to 20 million; and by the end of 1996 it had exploded to over 25 million. America is definitely on the move, the move back into the home as a place of doing business.

One of the most interesting aspects of this trend is the wide variety of men and women of all ages who are running home businesses. This group includes:

• People with minimal education to others with advanced college degrees;

• People with little or no business experience to seasoned corporate executives;

• People with very limited funds to those with sizable funding.

Virtually anyone can operate a business from home. All you need is an idea and the perseverance to bring that idea to reality. Follow the examples of home-based entrepreneurs such as the Wallaces, who published *Reader's Digest*; Bill Gates, who started Microsoft; and Mrs. Fields, who baked her way to fame with her homemade chocolate chip cookies.

Of course, you may not be expecting, or even desiring, your home business to grow into a huge enterprise. You may be someone who has chosen to work at a favorite hobby, and making money isn't your main concern. Or, you may want to make just enough money to live comfortably and not deal with the responsibilities of having employees.

You Can Be Your Own Boss

Having a home-based business gives you a freedom you wouldn't normally have in the working world. You answer to yourself. You take on as much or as little work as you like. You make your own schedule. You choose your own path. You are the boss.

If you are tired of seeing your smart ideas and hard work turn into money for someone else, or if you just want more flexibility in your schedule, why not start your own business at home? Others have. Perhaps you will recognize yourself in one of the groups of home-based entrepreneurs described below, or perhaps your situation is unique. Whatever your age, education, or financial status, you can start and run a business from home if you want — this book will show you the easiest road to realizing your dream.

Downsized Employees Can Work for Themselves

According to *The New York Times*, since the end of 1985, the total employment of Fortune 500 companies has declined by approximately two million employees. Are you one of those who was laid off? Perhaps you worked at a company that recently downsized, closed, or was forced into employee lay offs, and you feel that you can no longer give your loyalty to a company that treats you as a number. Your work experiences are valuable assets and can help you set up your own home-based business.

> Donna was a manager in charge of a 16-person department with an annual budget of more than two million dollars. However, when it came time to trim the company payroll, she lost her job, so she decided to take her years of experience and start a graphic design business at home. Today, with a lot less stress, Donna is earning about as much as she'd make working part-time in an office. Her initial investment included upgrading her computer system and making a lot of telephone calls to prospective clients. She now works as much as she can and still has time to tend a thriving vegetable garden.

Retirees Can Keep Active

As a retiree, you have valuable work and life experiences — as well as skills — that could easily be transferred into strong reasons for starting a home business. You may want to start a home business to simply fulfill your desire to stay busy and keep your mind active; to try out a great idea you've had under wraps all these years; to bring in extra income; or to market your homemade crafts.

With a home-based business you have the freedom to work only when you want to, so you can fit your business around your traveling, golf, playing with grand-children, and other activities you enjoy. Read about Neil and see how he made retirement work for him.

> Neil retired from his sales position shortly after suffering a heart attack. He didn't want to go back to work, but he had always been interested in crafts. He began spending his time creating jewelry and other small art objects. Soon, friends began asking him for his work, and he was on his way to a successful business at home. He now not only sells to friends, but has a small retail store following.

Parents Can Spend More Time with Their Children

Today many working parents would like to spend more quality time with their children. One way to accomplish this is to start a home business that offers a more flexible schedule. If you have school-age children and would like to be home when they are, perhaps you could arrange your business so you could be away from the house during school hours and be home in the afternoons.

> Vicky's two sons are in school during the day, so she takes in typing and other secretarial work during those hours, then puts her work aside when her children come home in the afternoon.

Perhaps you have small children and want to be home with them as much as possible. If you work at home, you can avoid day-care costs or just take your child to day care for part-days or a few days a week, so your child can socialize with others while you gain some quiet time.

> Sarah left her job as an editor on a large newspaper to stay at home with her new son. She used the contacts she had made in the newspaper business to set herself up as a freelance writer. Today, her son is five, and she has no plans for returning to work outside the home.

Professionals Can Control Their Workstyle

Many professionals, such as accountants, lawyers, doctors, dentists, engineers, architects, and other consultants run their businesses from home. They may actually perform their practice at home, and see clients and patients there. Or, they may do most of their work away from the home, but maintain an office at home where they do business activities such as marketing, recordkeeping, and billing.

> Milton was in his late 50s when his company decided to trim its work force and move to another state. He was not asked to move and decided to retire. Shortly after retiring, he began teaching in several colleges in the area, drawing on his more than 30 years of experience in the business world. Soon after, he decided to go back to school himself. Three years later, Milton passed the bar and became a lawyer. He now has a home-based career where he is his own boss and can decide when and if he wants to retire.

Seasonal Employees Can Boost Their Income at Home

If your primary employment is seasonal, you may want to use your off season to start a home-based business.

> Jake worked during summers as a builder and maintainer of swimming pools and hot tubs. His business was booming from late March to late October, but virtually dormant the rest of the year. During one winter, he decided to take a few woodworking classes to brush up his carpentry skills. By the end of the next season, he was making bookshelves and cabinets and found that working at home in the off season was very satisfying and profitable.

Tips for Making Work Suit Your Lifestyle

Tapping into the home-based business that best suits your lifestyle will take some time and effort on your part. So start slowly and keep these five tips in mind.

- **Keep to a Schedule.** During the course of a work day at home, all sorts of temptations can cross your path: television, snacks from the refrigerator, chats with friends on the phone, chores that need to be done around the house. When you are your own boss, there's no one watching to make sure you keep to a proper schedule. While a nine-to-five schedule may not be what you want, create some sort of schedule, and stick to it.

- **Set up a Separate Workspace.** Creating a workspace that is away from the daily activities in your home will keep your concentration from wandering. It will also help you more easily put your work aside while you relax with your family. There is nothing more disturbing than staring at a desk covered with work when you are in the family recreation room.

- **Avoid Socializing.** Neighbors, friends, and family members looking for something to do can be another cause for work-at-home distress. These people may assume you are available for socializing. While it may be fun at first to take the time to stop and talk with them, in the long run, it will cost you plenty in lost time and productivity. Remember, success comes from persistence, perseverance, and hard work. Learn to say no.

- **Join Networks and Professional Organizations.** Working at home can be lonely. This can be especially true for singles and retirees. There is no doubt that the workplace offers opportunities for socializing, and the shift to working at home can be isolating. To alleviate this isolation, one group of freelance editors formed a networking association. While these editors work from their own homes independently, they meet every other week to exchange ideas and network. On some projects, they choose to work in small groups. While these meetings are business-related, they also provide a boost for their morale.

Professional organizations have membership meetings all around the country. These can provide opportunities for exchanging ideas and gathering information. Trade shows and exhibits related to your field are also valuable events that will get you out of the house. And then, there's the business lunch with a colleague. No rule says that you have to stay home all the time with your nose to the grind stone. Get out and enjoy yourself once in a while; besides, it's a great way to let people know you are there, in case they may need your services one day or hear of someone else they can refer you to.

- **Get Your Family's Cooperation.** Your family members have to be on your side when you start your home business. Don't let them take you for granted. Just because you are at home does not mean that you are there to run all the household errands and chores. You will need the full cooperation of your family in order to keep going. If you find it hard to get the support you need, hold a family pow-wow and air your grievances. Come to a family compromise if needed, but at all costs, be sure your family understands and respects your schedule and responsibilities.

Mile Post

You may already have a great idea for your home-based business and just need to know how to proceed. Or, you may know how to proceed, but you need an idea. In either case, *Home Business Made Easy* will show you how to do both: Just follow its road and learn as you go.

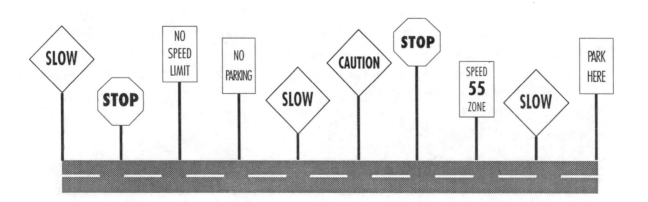

Chapter
1

Home Business Success Stories

Before learning how to explore your own work values, interests, and skills as well as select and start your own home-based business, you may want to read the six home business success stories in this chapter. These stories focus on entrepreneurs who are actively engaged in running successful home businesses in a variety of areas. By reading their experiences, you can gain valuable information and insight about how they selected, started, and currently operate their home-based businesses. Possibly, you can apply what you learn from this experience to your own situation. Although each business discussed below is different one from another, all of the entrepreneurs interviewed had certain things in common.

- They had the desire to be their own boss.
- They started out slowly on a part-time basis.

- They took time to test out their idea and did some market research before making an investment.
- They strived to keep overhead costs to a minimum.
- They found that the build-up time or growth was slower than anticipated.
- They had perseverance and persistence in reaching their goals.

International Distributorship

Mark worked most of his life in marketing and sales for a large manufacturing company. Often, when sitting around with his friends, he would talk of going off on his own. He dreamed of having his own business, and knew that if he did, it would somehow be related to marketing because that was the field in which he was most experienced.

Mark was also an avid sailor and he read every bit of information he could about sail boats and their accessories and equipment. Mark was particularly interested in power generators. One day, he came across an article about a foreign-made marine generator that appeared to out-perform anything he had seen offered in the United States. Intrigued by the product and recognizing its market potential in the United States, Mark called the manufacturer in Europe. Before he knew it, he was on his way across the Atlantic to speak with the owner of the company. He flew stand-by, of course, to keep those costs down! He came away with sole distribution rights to this marine generator in both the United States and Canada.

While gainfully employed on a full-time basis, Mark set up an office for his new venture in an empty bedroom in his house. He began to work evenings and weekends, creating brochures and placing ads in national boating magazines. As inquiries began to arrive in response to the ads, Mark sent out more and more brochures. Then the orders began to roll in.

Mark was able to fill his first orders from the limited inventory he had already purchased and kept warehoused in his office. Knowing that he had additional orders to fill, he was confident in placing larger orders with the manufacturer.

As time wore on and the market established by Mark grew, he was able to work out an agreement by which the foreign supplier agreed to help pay for advertising space in some of the major U.S. boating publications. This eventually led to attendance at marine industry trade shows around the country, where Mark's booth space was paid for by the supplier.

Today, Mark works full-time as a marketer of these marine generators and has increased his line to include additional marine products. From his sales, he has created an impressive mailing list, which he uses from time to time to send out direct-mail marketing materials or to announce new products. With each new order, Mark's list gets longer and provides a further incentive for suppliers to add their products to his growing inventory. He has moved his warehouse from the bedroom office to the family garage, in which he keeps only a three-month supply of product. This is part of an effort to keep overhead to a minimum.

When asked if he was happy with his new lifestyle, Mark couldn't have been more enthusiastic. He's finally his own boss; he can move around as freely as he wishes; his product line keeps him in close touch with his favorite hobby — sailing; and he has no more 35-mile commute to and from his office.

Mark's advice:

**Do your homework before you jump into any project. You don't want to
lose your investment.**

Illustration and Design Service

Not long ago, Joanne was working full-time for a small publishing company as the manager of its art design department. She had studied college-level illustration and had always dreamed of running a small illustration and design company from her home. But because she lived in a small apartment with her husband and they both needed to hold full-time jobs to keep up with the bills, she never knew when or how she should go out on her own.

When they decided to move into a house and to face their growing expenses, Joanne began to take jobs home to earn extra cash.

By starting slowly and purchasing the equipment she needed over a two-year period, Joanne worked her part-time venture into a full-time business that she now operates out of a spare bedroom in her home. She kept her initial investment low — about $2,000 for art equipment, drafting table, pens, waxer, etc.

While she covers costs for any outside materials or services up to $50, such as stats or special type, anything over $50 is billed directly from the supplier to the client. This, she explains, is done to keep overhead to a minimum. She also keeps her inventory of materials low, because tax laws allow deductions only on materials that have been used. For this reason, she buys what she needs on a job-by-job basis.

Most of Joanne's business is currently obtained through word-of-mouth recommendations. Initially, she did her homework and put her name in with the local printing and duplicating services in her area. She then researched those companies that would require the services she offered. Using her talent as an illustrator, she created a logo for her company and put together a packet of sample work which could be sent to prospective clients upon request. With the names and addresses obtained through her research, she did a small mailing to businesses in her area, enclosing a brief brochure and a business card that could be placed in an office Rolodex®. It was after this mailing that most of her requests for information came in. So far, Joanne has not needed to do another mailing because she has as much work as she can handle.

At first, Joanne felt lonely working out of her house. To alleviate this problem, she actively sought a few clients who would occasionally need her services in their offices. She also joined a network of freelance illustrators and regularly meets with them for brainstorming and networking sessions.

Joanne recently had a baby, which complicated her work schedule, but being able to work at home and be with her baby makes her very happy. After the baby was born, she limited her work hours and spread them out so she could work at her own convenience while the baby was napping. Now, however, she plans to use the services of a day-care or babysitting registry.

When asked how she was enjoying her new lifestyle, Joanne commented that it was just the way she had always envisioned it would be. Her time is flexible; if she feels stressed out by too much work, she can turn down a job or refer it to someone in her illustrators' network.

Joanne's advice:

Keep your overhead to a minimum and start slowly. This way, you won't make costly mistakes.

Bed and Breakfast

Ann and John are a retired couple in their late 60s who live in a large country home in a New York City suburb. The October 1987 stock market crash wiped out some of their savings and Ann and John had to consider selling their home to get enough cash to cover their bills and living expenses. Then one afternoon, Ann had lunch with a friend who talked about her husband's seminar series that was to take place later in the month. When her friend mentioned that the cost of hotel accommodations for out-of-town seminar attendees was very high, Ann suggested that for a small fee she could put someone up for the week in one of the three spare bedrooms in her home.

That was how it began. Today, Ann and John are registered with a large bed and breakfast association that periodically refers clients to them for short visits. With three available bedrooms and one bath, Ann and John are able to keep a good business going. If one person comes to stay in one of the single rooms and has private use of the bath because the two other rooms are vacant, the charge is $50 per night. If the double room is rented with private use of the bath, the charge is $80 per night. If the bathroom is shared, the rent is lowered to $35 per night for a single room and $50 per night for the double.

At first, Ann and John were concerned about opening their home to strangers. After the bed and breakfast association came to inspect their facilities, they were assured that they would be sent only screened clients. To this date, there have been no problems. As a matter of fact, Ann and John have gotten along so well with some of their guests that they have repeat clients. This is especially true of the people referred to them by their friends who run the seminar series.

When asked if people coming into their home cramped their lifestyle, Ann and John said no. Arrangements are made in advance; the length of the visit is decided upon; a time for the visitor's arrival is set; and a deposit is sent. The balance is paid on arrival. Ann prepares the room, supplying it with clean linens and towels. In the morning, she prepares a simple breakfast of fresh in-season fruit, baked goods, and coffee. Ann and John enjoy talking with their guests during this morning meal. At this time, they discuss the various restaurants and theaters in the area, and John gives them a small visitor's kit with maps and a list of suggested places to visit. Ann also noted that while she was required to clean the bathroom and supply fresh towels on a daily basis, all of her guests made their own beds.

Ann and John are happy; they have money coming into their home on a regular basis, nice people to talk to, and the flexibility to determine when and if they want to rent their rooms.

Ann and John's advice:

Don't give up; you never know where or how you may be able to get that extra money.

Catering Service

David and Drew are newlyweds who met through the catering business. Both are employed in full-time jobs, Drew in an office and as a freelance caterer and David as a chef at a country club. The couple is now starting up an independently run catering service out of their home.

David and Drew primarily cater to small parties held in private homes. David, being the chef of the operation, helps Drew prepare fancy appetizers and gourmet meals in their home kitchen. Drew meets with the clients to make arrangements for the upcoming party, giving advice on menu selections, decorations, and themes. Because they have many contacts in the restaurant field and can obtain additional help when necessary, it is easy for them to arrange for both large and small parties, though they prefer the more personal touch of the smaller party and plan to specialize in that area.

Their services include making arrangements with rental companies that supply tents, chairs, tables, and dinnerware. They also find or order party favors and other items requested by the party's host or hostess. With most of the food preparation being done in their home, David and Drew only supervise the serving of the food during the actual party. They hire outside personnel, such as bartenders and servers, only when the party's size warrants.

In many states, working with food requires special licensing and insurance. David and Drew made sure they had met all such licensing requirements.

So far, their investment has been minimal. Having just moved into a new house, they put most of their money into the kitchen, buying top-quality ovens, cooking utensils, and working counter space. For most of the parties they cater, a deposit is required upfront, with the remainder being paid on the day of the affair. For larger parties, the client is usually billed directly by the suppliers. This helps to keep the costs of overhead down.

Currently, David and Drew have no marketing plan other than word-of-mouth recommendations from satisfied customers, but they realize that eventually they will have to advertise if they want to expand their business. Though working long hours, David and Drew are happy and know this is the direction in which they want to go.

David and Drew's advice:

Expect to put in long hours when starting your own business.

Desktop Publishing

Peter began his home-based publishing business as a part-time venture while he was working full-time as an in-house staff writer for a large electronics corporation.

Like many editor/writers, Peter always wanted to work at home as a freelancer; however, it was difficult to build up a large enough client base to pay the household bills and living expenses. Examining freelance opportunities, Peter began to realize that more and more publishing companies were asking authors to submit manuscripts on computer disks rather than on mounds of type-written paper, and they were using freelance help to edit these manuscripts on disks. Having enough experience with computer word-processing software through his full-time job, Peter decided to invest in an IBM XT computer and a dot matrix printer. These would enable him to take freelance jobs and possibly arrange a work-at-home schedule with his current employer.

Shortly after Peter invested in the computer and the printer, he heard rumors that, because of financial problems, the company he worked for was planning layoffs and department closings, as well as cutbacks in the remaining areas. Because Peter had already considered arranging a work-at-home schedule, he decided that this was the ideal time to submit his proposal. His suggestion was accepted, and shortly thereafter, Peter was working happily at his old job (though at a reduced capacity) from his home.

With money coming in from a steady source, Peter began to research his options for increasing his cash flow. Using the public library as his greatest resource, Peter scanned directories to compile lists of publishing companies that might require his editorial services. Writing out each company name and address on a three-by-five-inch index card with appropriate contacts and brief company information, he soon had a list with which to begin his search for more clients.

Peter initiated contact with these publishing companies by composing a letter, which introduced himself and described the services he offered. Attached to the letter he included a brief questionnaire that asked what types of freelance services each company was seeking. With this, he also enclosed a self-addressed, stamped envelope. Peter found the returned questionnaires to be great time-saving devices because those companies taking the time to write back were the first companies he contacted with follow-up letters and phone calls.

He also discovered that his best potential customers were those who needed editing of manuscripts on computer disks.

Soon, Peter had several jobs that could be done easily on his computer. His initial investment had paid off. Peter then recognized another trend in the computer business — desktop publishing, which required the use of a high-quality laser printer and page-making software. Having experience with typesetting and page make-up, Peter decided to send out another questionnaire to determine how many companies would be interested in production services along with editorial work. This time, he used his computer to create a database of names and sent out letters and new questionnaires not only to publishers but to corporate communications departments as well. The response was as he expected. There was indeed a need for production services both in the publishing and corporate sectors.

Using money saved from his previous jobs, Peter invested approximately $5,000 in a laser printer that was capable of generating several type fonts and graphics.

He also invested about $1,000 in desktop publishing software that enabled him to create finished pages, not just manuscript pages that would need to be typeset elsewhere.

Using his new tools, he designed his own stationery and business cards and prepared a sample book that illustrated the different type fonts he could offer. Now, Peter could not only edit the material that was sent to him, but he could create the final copy as well.

Things were going well; Peter had plenty of clients; and he was earning more money than he had earned at his full-time job. But there was a problem — Peter could not possibly do all the work alone. To keep things flowing, he was forced to hire outside people to help with copy editing and proofreading. He also found the services of another work-at-home supplier useful — that of a neighbor who had turned her typing business into a wordprocessing venture. Being a slow typist himself, Peter found that by sending manuscripts out to be typed, he saved time and money. He simply includes the additional typing fee with his bill.

When asked if he enjoys working from his home, Peter said he did although he sometimes feels a sense of isolation from working alone. To counteract this, he has begun taking a karate class at a local school to get physical exercise and meet people.

Peter's advice:

Take the time to research any venture before getting started. Use questionnaires as part of the market research process.

Corporate Gift Service

A few years ago, Barbara and two other partners started a gift-buying service out of their homes.

Being housewives with grown children, the three partners decided they wanted to begin a venture that would bring in extra money; be operated out of their homes; enhance their lifestyles; and be fun. They got together a few times and brainstormed to come up with ideas for the business that would best suit these requirements. What they eventually decided upon was a gift-buying service.

Initially, Barbara and her two partners did a lot of individual buying for people they knew who needed gifts for weddings, showers, birthdays, graduations, and other special occasions. Their service quickly became popular by word-of-mouth. As time went on, however, they realized that customers who were corporate-based purchased in larger volume and were more likely to be repeat clients.

In an effort to increase their business in the corporate area, the partners invested in a mailing list and sent out a brochure in the form of an invitation for companies to "just pick up the phone" to use their services. This mailing worked and busy executives, who needed gifts for clients or employees, became steady customers.

Barbara and her partners do all the shopping, gift wrapping, and packing them-selves. Barbara maintains the company's office in her home, which includes a telephone answering machine for incoming orders or requests for information. One of her partners has set aside a basement area in her home, which is used as the company's gift wrapping and packing room.

One day, one of the owners of a public relations company asked for their help in obtaining a promotional item. The next thing they knew, their business had expanded into another exciting and lucrative area. Barbara and her partners not only zeroed in on that first promotional item, but they began working with other public relations firms, advertising agencies, and law firms as well, designing specialty items and finding manufacturers to produce them.

This led them to developing a product for the public relations firm of a well-known television personality. They took the theme of a new television program and had a manufacturer emboss a slogan on a specially manufactured gift box which was mailed to television stations through the United States. The public relations firm has become a regular customer for personalized items for several of their television personalities.

Later an advertising agency was looking for an item to mail to potential clients. Barbara and her partners created a four inch attaché case filled with information about the agency which was used to attract new clients. From gift buying for friends and relatives, they were now dealing with television personalities, heads of large advertising agencies, and managing partners of law firms.

When a request for items is received, the client is asked to set a price range. The partners then gather ideas for gift items in this range and make a presentation. When the client decides on a particular item, a 50% deposit is requested from new accounts. For standing clients, the deposit is usually waived and full payment is required on delivery.

The gifts are purchased wholesale. One of the company's primary selling points is its resale prices, which are 15% to 20% below retail. The size of the discount passed on to their customers depends on the size of the order and how competitive the item might be at retail.

To keep overhead to a minimum, Barbara and her partners never warehouse items. They do most of their shopping at a merchandise center located in a nearby city, which houses more than 100 manufacturers that sell gifts at wholesale prices. Attendance at trade and gift shows, as well as stationery and merchandising shows, have also proved to be a valuable way to get gift ideas.

As buyers, Barbara and her partners have spent many pleasant working afternoons browsing through these shows, talking with dealers, making contacts, and picking up product catalogs. In addition, they maintain a library of product catalogs and brochures for generating new ideas.

When asked if she enjoyed working from her home, Barbara remarked that her gift-buying service is a perfect complement to her family and outside activities. She is able to work part-time doing something she enjoys.

Barbara's advice:

Keep your initial investment and your overhead low, take your time, know what you want to do, make sure you will like to do it, and have fun.

After reading these success stories, you may have noted that these successful home-based businesses were started by people with a variety of skills and interests who simply had the perseverance to make their ideas work.

Mile Post

You, too, have the skills, talents, and experiences to start your own home-based business. Add perseverance to the business idea and you'll be on your way.

Chapter
2

Explore Your Work Values, Interests, and Skills

If you ask home business owners why they started their particular business, you will hear a variety of responses ranging from wanting to be their own boss to fulfilling a life-long dream. Before you begin your own home business, you need to explore the reasons why you want to start your own business and see how your particular strengths and personality can help you create a successful business.

By completing the self-assessment exercises in this chapter, you will gain a better understanding regarding your work values, interests, and skills — important considerations for any career choice — and you will develop some guidelines for determining how to choose one home business idea over another.

So, pick up a pencil and take a little time to complete the easy-to-follow exercises in this chapter. You may find your results unexpectedly interesting.

Work Values

Work values reflect what you feel is most important to you when you think about work and what you want to get out of it. For example, two people may want to be teachers, but for very different reasons. One may value the opportunity to nurture young people and watch them develop, while another may enjoy the intellectual stimulation that comes from being an expert in a particular subject area. When you think about starting a business, is your motivation to serve others; to gain financial independence; to add some variety to your life; or is it a combination of all of these? With work values, there are no right or wrong answers, just your own preferences.

The list below contains some common values that many people look for to provide motivation in their work. Try ranking these values from 1 to 16, according to their importance to you.

____	Achievement	____	Power
____	Challenge	____	Recognition
____	Creativity	____	Risk/excitement
____	High status	____	Security
____	Independence	____	Self-expression
____	Interesting work	____	Service to others
____	Leadership	____	Socializing
____	Material comfort	____	Variety

What values did you rank highest? _____
_____
_____

What values did you rank lowest? _____
_____
_____

Did you learn anything new about yourself by doing this exercise?

_____
_____
_____

Did any of these values stand out clearly as most important, or were all the choices difficult?

_____
_____

People often leave jobs and start new careers because of value conflicts or because their values have changed and they no longer get the satisfaction that they used to from a particular job or type of work. Keep these value choices in mind as you go through the rest of this chapter.

Interests

Interests are activities you enjoy doing, regardless of your skill level. Many people enjoy sports, for example, whereas only a few actually earn a living as professional athletes. To identify your areas of interest, make a list of those things you like to do both at work and in your spare time. Try to compile a list of at least 15 to 20 enjoyable activities.

Enjoyable Activities for You:

_____	_____
_____	_____
_____	_____
_____	_____
_____	_____
_____	_____
_____	_____
_____	_____
_____	_____

Next, see if these activities fall into any obvious categories, such as activities you like to do with others versus those you like to do alone. Based on what you like to do, are there a number of activities that involve doing things with your hands, such as sewing or cooking? Or are you more of a people person who enjoys doing things in groups with others, such as playing cards or singing in a choir?

In the space provided below, choose two categories and separate your list of enjoyable activities accordingly.

_____ **Activities:**   _____ **Activities:**

_____   _____

_____   _____

_____   _____

_____   _____

_____   _____

_____   _____

_____   _____

_____   _____

_____   _____

_____   _____

To help you get a different perspective on any possible pattern of your interests, show your list of enjoyable activities to a friend or family member. Their responses may shed a new light on how you view your interest pattern.

Skills

Strong skills are often related to your interests because you tend to develop and improve your skills in areas where you enjoy spending your time; however, it is possible to have skills in areas that you don't necessarily enjoy.

One of the best ways to identify your "motivated skills"— those skills you like to use most — is to make a list of the things you consider at this point in time to be your life's accomplishments and see which skills you needed most to accomplish them. Life accomplishments can be defined as things you enjoy doing, you do very well, and of which you are proud. These accomplishments do not have to be major achievements, but they should have meaning for you and provide a sense of satisfaction. You may find it helpful to list accomplishments by thinking about things you did at different ages, such as from 5 to 10 years old, 20 to 35 years old, or 40 to 60 years old. Here are some examples.

> "The summer job I had when I was 16 was very important to me. I worked in a store selling shoes and realized that I had a knack for getting along with all different kinds of people."

> "I recently took a Chinese cooking class and tried out the recipes on some friends. They loved the food and said that I had a real knack for making the food look as good as it tasted."

> "I started fixing TV sets when I was in high school and now friends and family call me when they have problems with their electronic equipment."

At this time, on a separate piece of paper, develop an overall list of 15 to 20 life accomplishments from different areas of your life, such as school, work, and leisure activities. If you have family members around, perhaps they can help you remember some accomplishments from your early years.

Once you have your list of accomplishments, identify what your motivated skills are by grouping your accomplishments under the six skill groups listed below. Read through these skill groups before completing the Motivated Skills worksheet on page 25.

- **Personal/helping skills.** These skills involve helping and supporting others. People who enjoy using these skills are usually sensitive to their own feelings and to the feelings of others. They are likely to be asked for help by family or friends who need a hand or support with some problem.

- **Managing/leading skills.** These skills involve managing projects or people and obtaining results. Managers usually enjoy organizing, leading, and influencing those around them and are likely to find themselves being chosen to lead groups in which they become involved.

- **Technical/scientific skills.** These skills involve using scientific methods and equipment to solve problems and understand the world. Scientific thinkers like complicated problems and are curious about how things work.

- **Creative/artistic skills.** These skills involve self-expression and creativity, usually in some artistic medium, such as painting, writing, or theater. Artists usually have their own way of doing or seeing things and are quite sensitive to sounds, colors, and textures.

- **Organizing/detail skills.** These skills involve keeping things in order and following through until a job is done thoroughly and completely. People with these skills are good at organizing projects and getting things done on time.
- **Building/mechanical skills.** These skills involve being good with one's hands and include an ability to analyze and solve practical problems. People with these skills are good at working with machines and tools and building or repairing things.

To complete the Motivated Skills worksheet, take each accomplishment on your life accomplishment list on the preceding page and place it under the skill group you used most in completing that particular accomplishment. If there is an accomplishment you feel used more than one skill group, list that accomplishment under the appropriate skill group headings.

For example, if you wrote down "managing a Little League baseball team" on your accomplishments list, you might enter that under these three skill groups:

- Managing/Leading Skills — you kept the kids focused on the game.
- Personal/Helping Skills — you helped each of the kids improve his playing ability and self-image.
- Organizing/Detail Skills — you arranged car pools and organized fundraisers.

When you have finished placing each of your accomplishments on the worksheet, it should indicate which of these skill groups are your strongest skills and which are your weakest. Your motivated skills are the skill groups with the most accomplishments listed, while your weaker skill groups have fewer accomplishments.

Motivated Skills Worksheet

Personal/Helping Skills

_____

_____

_____

_____

_____

_____

Managing/Leading Skills

_____

_____

_____

_____

_____

_____

Technical/Scientific Skills

_____

_____

_____

_____

_____

Creative/Artistic Skills

_____

_____

_____

_____

_____

Organizing/Detail Skills

_____

_____

_____

_____

_____

_____

Building/Mechanical Skills

_____

_____

_____

_____

_____

_____

Now that you have gone through some self-assessment activities, you have a better idea about the work values, interests, and skills that you may be trying to express by setting up a home business. Write a brief summary of what you have learned about yourself in each of these three areas.

My work values are:

_____

_____

_____

_____

My interests are:

_____

_____

_____

_____

_____

My skills are:

_____

_____

_____

_____

_____

Select a Business to Suit Your Strengths

As you consider the home businesses described throughout this book, you'll notice that they generally fall into two categories — service businesses and product businesses.

Service

Service businesses can be divided into two categories.

- Those that help people directly with some aspect of their lives, such as house cleaning or dog walking; and
- Those that teach people some skill, such as cooking lessons or computer tutoring.

In terms of work values, interests, and skills, people who are drawn to service-focused businesses most likely value providing a service to others, enjoy closeness and social contact, and have good interpersonal skills. Those who choose to teach may also be leaders who have some strong interest or well-developed skill that they want to share with others.

Product

As will be discussed in Chapter 5, product businesses can also be divided into two categories.

- Those that sell and distribute products created by others; and
- Those that have the creator of the product do the selling.

People who are drawn to the distribution businesses are likely to be strong organizers or managers who may be expressing a wide variety of values and interests through the organizations they set up. Those who produce goods for sale will often have a special skill or talent and will value creativity and independence in their work.

For more information on service and product businesses, see Chapter 5.

Mile Post

After exploring your work values, interests, and skills, and determining where your strengths are in terms of a product or service business, you will be able to further identify those business areas that suit you best.

Chapter
3

Select the Right Business for You

When you decide to start a home-based business, one of the most difficult decisions will be to select a business that is right for you. To help you with this decision, work your way through the selection process which is discussed and outlined in this chapter. This selection process — or road to success — will guide you through the three main steps necessary to selecting your final business idea.

1. Identify potential businesses.

2. Reduce number of potential businesses.

3. Arrive at your final selection.

Before starting your journey through the selection process — which follows with various worksheets and instructions — review the illustration on the following pages for a quick overview.

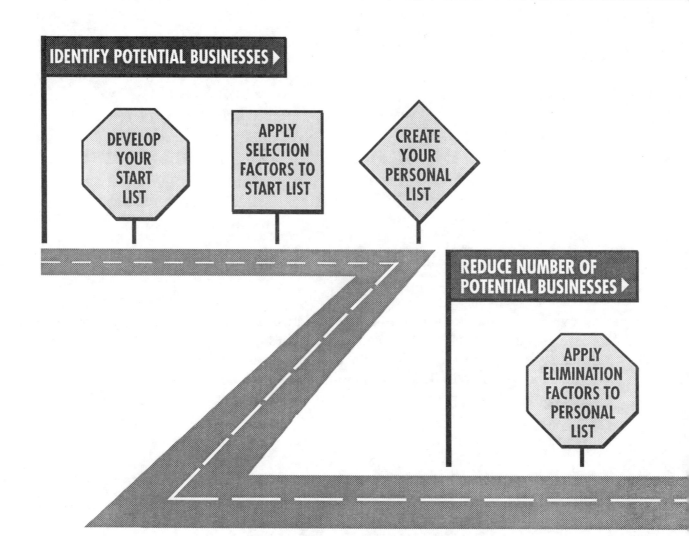

IDENTIFY POTENTIAL BUSINESSES ▶

DEVELOP YOUR START LIST

APPLY SELECTION FACTORS TO START LIST

CREATE YOUR PERSONAL LIST

REDUCE NUMBER OF POTENTIAL BUSINESSES ▶

APPLY ELIMINATION FACTORS TO PERSONAL LIST

Easy Steps for Selecting Your Home Business

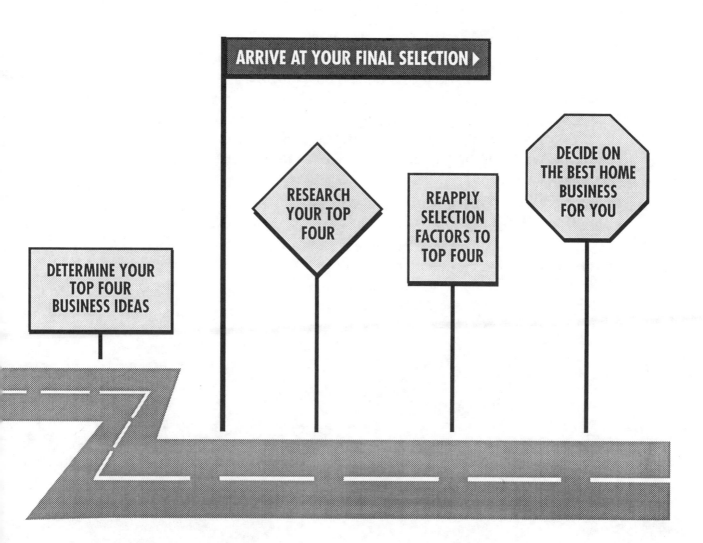

ARRIVE AT YOUR FINAL SELECTION ▶

RESEARCH YOUR TOP FOUR

REAPPLY SELECTION FACTORS TO TOP FOUR

DECIDE ON THE BEST HOME BUSINESS FOR YOU

DETERMINE YOUR TOP FOUR BUSINESS IDEAS

When deciding which business is right for you, many factors have to be taken into consideration — some more important than others.

Some which you may consider important at first can change in their importance as a result of other factors coming into play.

> As an example, you may plan to devote a limited amount of time to a new business so that it will not interfere with your family life. To achieve this, you have to hire a deliveryperson. If your planned investment does not allow for hiring such a person, you have the choice of either devoting more time to the business by becoming the deliveryperson in addition to everything else; increasing your planned investment by paying for the deliveryperson; or choosing another business.

> Your planned investment is the amount of money you have decided you can comfortably afford in order to start your home-based business. Increasing your planned investment at the spur of the moment can lead you to the uncomfortable position of being too far in debt. Having the proper capital to get your business off the ground is one of the most important aspects of your start up.

The selection process should go on until you make a single, final choice. Remember, there is no right or wrong selection — just your own preference and what seems right for you. Keeping this in mind, get a pen or pencil and start down the road to selecting success.

Identify Potential Businesses

The first step in the selection process is to identify potential business ideas you feel are right for you. The exercises in this initial step are to:

- Develop your start list.
- Apply selection factors to start list.
- Create your personal list.

Develop Your Start List

In the space provided below, list any business ideas you would like or feel confident about starting. To help give you ideas on various types of businesses, refer to Chapter 8. Remember to include any favorable business ideas or suggestions from family members or business-oriented magazines. The number of businesses selected for your start list can be as long as you like. Even if you are in doubt about the business idea, put it on your start list.

Your Start List of Business Ideas

_____ _____ _____

_____ _____ _____

_____ _____ _____

_____ _____ _____

_____ _____ _____

_____ _____ _____

Apply Selection Factors to Start List

After compiling your start list, you need to consider five important factors when selecting your home-based business. They are:

- **Enjoyment.** Will you find this business enjoyable?
- **Lifestyle.** Will this business fit into your business, home, and social lifestyles?
- **Time.** Do you have the time required to run this business?
- **Investment.** Do you have enough money to start this business?
- **Income.** Is the expected income adequate for your needs?

To apply these five major selection factors to each of the businesses on your start list, make enough copies of the Selection Factors worksheet — which is shown on page 7 — so you can write down each business idea from your start list on the top line labeled "business". Then, below each business idea, write a brief description of the business. In this description, jot down what and how you will be manufacturing, offering, or retailing your product or service. Try to be as specific as possible. It will help you to quickly answer the selection factor questions listed above by simply checking the "yes" or "no" boxes provided at the side of each business description.

Initially, you may not have sufficient information about each business to determine to what degree the five selection factors apply to each business. Nevertheless, use your instincts, best judgment, and "gut feeling" in applying these factors. If necessary, go through your start list a few times and reapply the selection factors. Delete business ideas that do not have "yes" answers for all five selection factors.

Selection Factors Worksheet

Business _____

Factors	**Yes**	**No**
Enjoyment	☐	☐
Lifestyle	☐	☐
Time	☐	☐
Investment	☐	☐
Income	☐	☐

Description _____
_____
_____
_____
_____

Business _____

Factors	**Yes**	**No**
Enjoyment	☐	☐
Lifestyle	☐	☐
Time	☐	☐
Investment	☐	☐
Income	☐	☐

Description _____
_____
_____
_____
_____

Business _____

Factors	**Yes**	**No**
Enjoyment	☐	☐
Lifestyle	☐	☐
Time	☐	☐
Investment	☐	☐
Income	☐	☐

Description _____
_____
_____
_____
_____

Create Your Personal List

When you have completed a Selection Factors worksheet for each business idea on your start list and tossed those with less than five "yes" answers, your start list has now been reduced to what is called your personal list. Write these business selections in the space provided below.

The number of businesses selected from your start list for your personal list can be as long as you like, but it should contain at least ten businesses. If you have a problem with selecting ten businesses from your start list, lessen the intensity when applying the selection factors. As an example:

> "I think I would enjoy this business." versus "I know I would enjoy this business."
>
> "I believe it will fit my lifestyle."versus "It definitely fits my lifestyle."

Your Personal List of Business Selections

_____   _____

_____   _____

_____   _____

_____   _____

_____   _____

_____   _____

_____   _____

Reduce Number of Potential Businesses

The next step in the selection process of a home-based business is to eliminate businesses from your personal list that may not be as right for you as others. To complete this second step:

- Apply elimination factors to personal list.
- Determine your top four business ideas.

Apply Elimination Factors to Personal List

To help you reduce the number of business ideas from your personal list, review the ten elimination factors listed below. These factors and questions will prove useful when judging business ideas against one another, and they should be used to check the appropriate "yes" or "no" answer box on the Elimination Factors worksheet on page 39.

- **Training.** If special training is required, do you have the training or are you able to obtain it?
- **Growth.** Is there any growth potential for the business?
- **Education.** If special education is necessary, do you have this education or are you able to obtain it?
- **Risk.** Is the projected financial risk something you can afford?
- **Interests.** Does the business reflect your personal interests?
- **Space.** Is the required space for the business available and adequate?

- **Experience.** Will any of your previous work experiences contribute to the business?
- **Schedules.** Is the required scheduling acceptable?
- **Strength.** If physical strength is required, can you handle it?
- **Skill.** If any special skill is needed to run the business, do you have such a skill or are you able to obtain it?

For each of the businesses on your personal list, complete the exercise outlined on the Elimination Factors worksheet on the opposite page. Be sure to make extra copies of the worksheet if you have several business ideas to review.

On the Elimination Factors worksheet, list all the business ideas from your personal list and answer the questions outlined above regarding the ten elimination factors by checking the "yes" or "no" box under each business idea. As you did when applying the selection factors to your start list, toss any business ideas that do not have ten unanimous "yes" answers.

Use your best judgment and instincts when applying the elimination factors to businesses on your personal list. Bear in mind that these factors are used to eliminate businesses, not to select them.

As an example, in reviewing a particular business on your personal list, you may feel that special training will be necessary. If you do not have the training or will not be able to obtain it, eliminate that business when applying the training factor. If the business requires physical strength and you are not physically able to supply it, eliminate that business when you come to the strength factor.

Elimination Factors Worksheet

Business:

	Yes No		Yes No		Yes No		Yes No		Yes No
Training	☐ ☐	**Education**	☐ ☐	**Interests**	☐ ☐	**Experience**	☐ ☐	**Strength**	☐ ☐
Growth	☐ ☐	**Risk**	☐ ☐	**Space**	☐ ☐	**Schedules**	☐ ☐	**Skill**	☐ ☐

Summary

_____

_____

Business:

	Yes No		Yes No		Yes No		Yes No		Yes No
Training	☐ ☐	**Education**	☐ ☐	**Interests**	☐ ☐	**Experience**	☐ ☐	**Strength**	☐ ☐
Growth	☐ ☐	**Risk**	☐ ☐	**Space**	☐ ☐	**Schedules**	☐ ☐	**Skill**	☐ ☐

Summary

_____

_____

Business:

	Yes No		Yes No		Yes No		Yes No		Yes No
Training	☐ ☐	**Education**	☐ ☐	**Interests**	☐ ☐	**Experience**	☐ ☐	**Strength**	☐ ☐
Growth	☐ ☐	**Risk**	☐ ☐	**Space**	☐ ☐	**Schedules**	☐ ☐	**Skill**	☐ ☐

Summary

_____

_____

Determine Your Top Four Business Ideas

If, after doing this elimination application, you have more than four business ideas remaining from your personal list, you must reevaluate and reapply one of the ten elimination factors — interest. Interest is the most important elimination factor to consider when evaluating business ideas because if a business idea does not reflect your interests, you will not enjoy the work; the business will not fit into your lifestyle; and your overall mental outlook toward the business will not enhance your chances for success.

So, in the "Summary" space provided on the Elimination Factors worksheet, detail how your interest applies to the business idea you are considering by determining:

- Your interest level in the business idea; and
- How much you will enjoy the business activities.

Use this application and introspection to reduce your personal list to your final top four business ideas.

Your Top Four Business Ideas

1. _____

2. _____

3. _____

4. _____

Arrive at Your Final Selection

With this third step, you are in the homestretch of making your final business selection. The exercises included in this last step are:

- Research your top four.
- Reapply selection factors to top four.
- Decide on the best home business for you.

Research Your Top Four

To make an informed decision regarding your final business selection and learn more about your top four business ideas, take the time to do some research. Find out as much as possible about each business idea. Ask yourself questions, such as:

- How many competitors are in your area?
- What will be your target market?
- How many months after the business starts can you anticipate having income?
- What sort of price or fee should you ask for your product or service?
- How much time will you have to commit to start the business?
- What licensing fees and requirements will your business need?
- What should you expect to pay for start-up costs?
- What is the demand for this product or service?
- Will you need to hire employees?

To get answers to these questions, you can begin with your local library's reference desk. The reference desk can direct you to local business resources and directories. The library will also have collections of business magazines, where you can research trends and how-to information. Business books written by professionals and experts are other good research sources you'll find at the library. Don't forget your friends and family. They often have had various business experiences that can help provide useful insight into your top four selections.

You may also want to visit your local Small Business Development Center (SBDC). The SBDC network is a program between the U.S. Small Business Administration and your state's higher education system. Using their combined resources, these two organizations provide small business consulting; conduct business-oriented workshops; and publish a variety of free small business publications covering an array of topics. To contact your state's SBDC office, refer to the SBDC list in Appendix C. The state SBDC office on this list can tell you where to find the SBDC nearest you.

Another good starting point would be to check with your state's economic development or commerce departments. These government agencies often have small business specialists available to anyone interested in starting a business in the state.

Finally, to get more information and insight into your business idea, contact an owner of a similar existing business. This type of networking will benefit you in your research and possibly in the future.

For any financial questions or issues you'd like to research at this point, the section on estimating your investment in Chapter 4 might be of assistance.

Reapply Selection Factors to Top Four

After completing your research on your top four business ideas, you may already have eliminated a business or two from the list. At the very least, you should have an idea of what each business may require and how complex or easy the start up may be for you.

To reduce the top four to a final one, reapply the selection factors — outlined in the first step of identifying your potential businesses — to the top four. Use the Selection Factors worksheet provided earlier to accomplish this.

Feel free to discuss your top four selections with friends and family, but remember, this final decision is to select the best business for you, not a friend or family member.

Decide on the Best Home Business for You

After reapplying the selection factors, discussing the selection with others, and taking your research into consideration, determine your final business selection and write it down in the space provided.

Your Final Business Selection: _____

Mile Post

Congratulations! You have just completed one of the more difficult processes you'll ever face as a new business owner.

Now that you have decided on which business to start you are ready for the information in the next chapter — start-up steps.

Chapter
4

Start-up Steps for Your Home Business

Now that you have completed the selection process and have decided which home business is right for you, you probably have many questions about how to get your business started. To help you know where to start and possibly answer some of your questions, ten important steps for starting your new home-based business are shown on the road illustration on pages 46 and 47.

As you read about each of these ten start-up steps and what they entail, make note as to what you will need to complete for your particular business. Bear in mind that because there is virtually an endless number of possible home-based businesses, there may be some unique start-up aspects for your particular business that are not covered in the road illustration and the subsequent start-up step discussions.

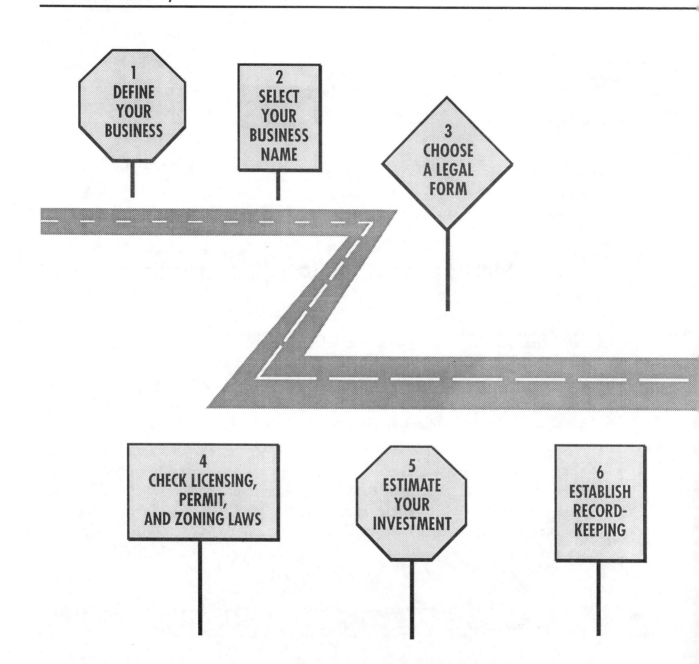

Ten Easy Steps Down the Road to Starting Your Home Business

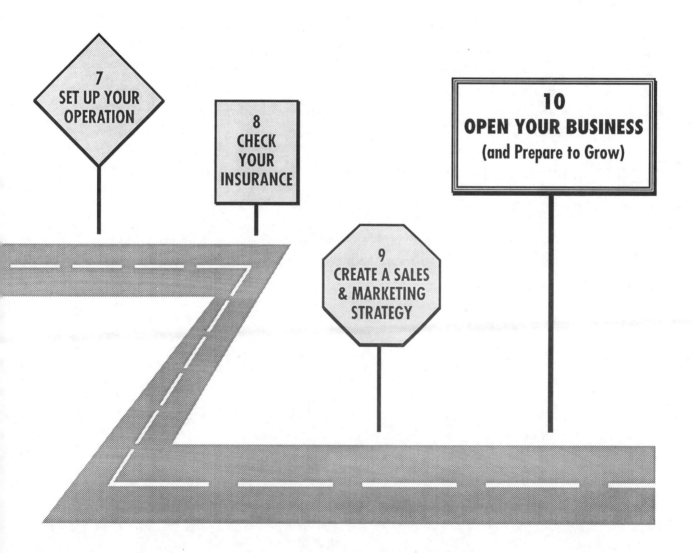

To address these unique issues, contact your local Small Business Development Center (SBDC), as listed in Appendix C, or your state economic development department. Or you could talk with your accountant, attorney, or small business consultant.

You may also want to obtain a copy of a book called *Starting and Operating a Business in* (your state) from your local book source or from The Oasis Press at (800) 228-2275. The *Starting and Operating a Business* series, with its custom editions for each of the 50 states and the District of Columbia, explains specific federal and state requirements and directs you to sources of information about permits and licenses. This comprehensive book also features a wealth of general how-to information for any business owner in any state. This publication is updated annually with the newest changes in laws and taxes that affect small businesses. It would be an excellent resource for detailing the ten start-up steps outlined in this chapter.

Also, you may want to get in touch with the Home Business Institute at 1-888-DIAL-HBI to see how this national membership organization might assist you in getting started.

Define Your Business

To clarify the purpose, direction, and objective of your new business, put them in writing. In so doing, you make it easier to address the essential points — such as pricing, competition, work space, investment, equipment, sales strategy, profit, and growth potential — you need to consider as you start your new home-based business. Defining your business can be challenging and will require some extra effort, however, this exercise will help you get your business started and operating more smoothly and efficiently, and possibly point out some important aspects that you might miss.

To begin, describe the product(s) or service(s) your business will offer; to whom; at what price; and in what geographical area. Ask these questions:

- How much space will you need?
- How much will it cost to provide the product(s) or service(s)?
- What investment will be necessary?
- What type of marketing plan will you use to sell your product(s) or service(s)?
- What do you expect your profit and growth potential to be?

Do as much investigation as you can and use your best judgment to arrive at a concise and clear definition of your business.

Before you write your business definition, read through each of the remaining start-up steps so you get an idea of the areas your business definition should cover. After you have completed your definition, go through each start-up step again and determine any actions you should take and any decisions you should make before starting your business. To help you get started on your own definition, take a look at this example.

Business Definition Example

Assume you intend to make wooden mailboxes which you will sell to local hardware, houseware, and variety stores. You will sell your mailboxes for $30 each to stores within a 20-mile radius of your home. You will call on the store owners yourself, show them a sample mailbox and solicit orders. Your basement workshop has sufficient equipment to manufacture the mailboxes so no new equipment will be necessary. You estimate that materials will cost about seven dollars per mailbox and you can make 15 mailboxes per week in your spare time. At that rate of production, your investment for materials will average $105 per week. Eventually, you intend to increase the time you spend working at your new business so you can expand the marketing area. If you worked full-time, you estimate you could make 70 mailboxes per week, which would require $490 per week for materials.

In this example, you have defined several detailed aspects of your wooden mailbox manufacturing company. But, did you check to see if there was any competition in your local area? It was missed in the example shown. Be sure to address all aspects of the nine remaining start-up steps in your definition, plus any others you feel apply to your particular business selection. Remember, this initial step will help you investigate what it is going take to get your business started and operating. Define your own business now on a separate piece of paper.

Select Your Business Name

If you think choosing a name for your new business will be easy — think again! If you are like most people, you will probably find that choosing a name that conveys your new product or service in a positive, attractive, and creative way is a difficult task. Nevertheless, it is a very important task because your company's name is likely to be the first piece of information a prospective customer will learn about your business. The name can have a lasting positive or negative effect.

A good business name can be an attention getter and a no-cost means of advertising; however, experts themselves do not agree on what constitutes a good business name. Should the name:

- Convey exactly what the business does — Home Catering Company?
- Be playful — Pete's Eats?
- Be serious — Standard Laundry Supplies?
- Include a family name — Jones Messenger Service?
- Include a geographical location — Ohio Novelties?

You may want to have your business' name convey a message, perhaps by incorporating one or more of the following points in the name:

- Your product or service — Creative Catering;
- Your business location — Brook Avenue Woodworking;
- Your marketing area — Southern Distribution; or
- An appropriate descriptive word — "reliable," "speedy," "durable," or "elegant."

While considering various possibilities, keep in mind the type of customers you will be targeting.

- Would they be more likely to respond positively to a whimsical or catchy name; or

- Would they be more likely to respond positively to a name that is more serious or conservative?

Avoid names that are too specific. For example, "Artistic Wreaths" would be a better name than "Artistic Christmas Wreaths," because the latter name implies that the business only manufactures Christmas wreaths. Also avoid using initials in your company name, such as "RDL Caterers." Such names tend to be easily forgotten.

While the experts discourage using family names, if your business will be confined to an area where your family is well known and respected, it might actually be an asset to use your family name. In most cases, you should avoid using a family name if it is difficult to pronounce, spell, or remember. There are always, of course, exceptions to every rule.

In the space provided on the next page, jot down your business name ideas.

After you have thought of several names for your new home-based business, get the reactions of family members and friends. In the end, however, you must be the judge of which name you are the most comfortable with and which best suits your business.

Your Business Name Ideas:

_____   _____

_____   _____

_____   _____

_____   _____

_____   _____

_____   _____

_____   _____

_____   _____

_____   _____

_____   _____

_____   _____

After you have decided on a name, it should be registered with the proper agency, most likely your secretary of state's office. If there is another business with the exact name (or a very similar name), you will have to chose another name. It is important to register your company's name to protect and prevent it from being used in the future by some other company.

Choose a Legal Form of Business

Three choices for organizing your business are available in any state. They are the sole proprietorship, the partnership, and the corporation.

When deciding on which legal form of business organization you will use for your new home-based business, ask yourself the following questions:

- Do you want to limit your liability for business losses, or are you willing to assume the risk to the full extent of your personal net worth?

- Do you think you will want or need to seek money from investors? If so, do you want them to have an ownership interest in the business and a say in the operation of the business?

- What are the tax consequences of operating your business as a sole proprietorship, partnership, or corporation? Is there a choice that will minimize the amount of taxes you will be required to pay?

- How much money do you want to spend on legal and related costs to organize your business? How much time?

- Is it important that ownership of your business be freely transferable?

- Does the form of business organization you select involve formalities, such as requiring periodic meetings and the preparation of legal documents?

Keep your business organization simple. If you can get legal advice at a very reasonable cost, take it. This initial investment may save you money in the long run.

Keep in mind that it is more important to get your business organized and running than it is to plan for eventualities that may never occur. Use common sense.

If you are starting your home-based business on your own, you will most likely be best served by organizing as a sole proprietorship. If you plan to have a partner, then a partnership is the obvious choice of organization. If you want to limit your business liabilities and still pay only one set of taxes on your profits, try a Subchapter S corporation. At this point, the least desirable organizational model for your small business would be a regular corporation. For more information on legal forms of business organization, refer to Chapter 6.

Check Licensing, Permit, and Zoning Regulations

Certain licensing, permit, and zoning regulations may apply to the business you are planning to operate. For some businesses, it will be a simple matter to comply with the applicable regulations, while for others, it may be a formidable task. Much depends on the nature of your home-based business, the neighborhood you live in, and local and state ordinances. In any case, the burden of complying with these and other regulations will fall upon you. It is up to you to determine what regulations apply in order to operate the business you have chosen. Failure to do so could result in penalties, an interruption of your business, or even having to move or abandon the business.

Before starting operations, contact your city or town hall or any other appropriate regulatory agency for information. If there is a sales tax to be levied, make sure you contact the proper authorities to determine what your responsibilities are. If you are conducting a business which renders certain services — such as a beautician, cosmetologist, barber, real estate broker, investment adviser, insurance agent, mechanic, electrician, or plumber — you may need an occupational license from a state regulatory agency. Businesses that make or distribute food may need the approval of the local health department. Child-care services may also require special licensing. Many states have one-stop permit centers that should be able to help answer any licensing, permit, or zoning questions. Check your local telephone listings for such an agency.

Depending on the business you choose, you may need zoning approval to operate it from your home. It is unlikely that you will need any zoning approval if you are just operating a simple office from one of your spare rooms. However, if you are setting up a small assembly line to manufacture pottery that requires potter's wheels, baking ovens, and a conveyor, you should make sure that you are not violating any zoning regulations in your area. Obviously, some common sense applied in this regard will keep you out of trouble. If what you will be doing from your home is going to annoy your neighbors and be a detriment to your neighborhood, you may be looking for trouble if you don't thoroughly check out the zoning requirements. If large trucks will be delivering merchandise to your garage, or the present traffic pattern in your area will change as a result of your home-based business, you will probably be hearing from your neighbors or some political figure in your area, asking you to cease and desist.

Another area that should be checked thoroughly is signage. You may be limited as to the signs you can put on your property. Use good judgment and check out applicable laws.

If your business seems to require no special licensing or if you are confident that you have complied with regulations, then hop to it and start running your business. But if you have any doubts, consult a lawyer, accountant, or other professional for advice.

Estimate Your Investment

Every new business needs some money to start operating. Yours is no exception. You'll need to answer several important questions relating to money before you launch your business:

- How much money will you need to invest in the business?

- Over what period of time will you need it until the business earns enough to repay the investment?

- What monies will be necessary for you and your family to live on while you are getting your new business off the ground?

- Where will this money come from — from your present job, savings, your spouse's income, an outside source, or from a combination of these?

- What operational costs are likely, such as, phone, utility bills, and insurance?

- What supplies will be necessary?

- What assets, such as equipment or furniture, must you acquire?

- What promotional materials or ads will you need to get the business off the ground, and what will they cost?

- Have you provided for important items, such as health insurance?

- Can you get some funding from outside sources?

To answer these questions, you will need to make up two budgets: a household budget and a business budget. The information and worksheets on the next few pages will walk you through creating these essential business tools.

Household Budget

The household budget includes all the normal family and personal expenses and income you expect for one year.

Use your checkbook, credit card statements, and other records to determine the total your household spent on all family and personal items last year. Next, project what those same items will cost for the next year and enter your projections on the Household Budget worksheet on the next page.

The amounts in your projection should be the same or close to the previous year's unless you anticipate a substantial change for some items, such as increased expenses for a new baby or college tuition, or a decrease due to paying off a loan or mortgage.

Now write down your total anticipated household income — not counting what you expect from your new home business. Then deduct the total expenditures that you just tallied.

If your anticipated household income is greater than your expenditures, your result will be a positive number indicating you will have a surplus available to invest in your new business. However, if your result is a negative number, you will have a deficiency. You'll need to cover this deficiency with income from your business or other sources in order to meet your anticipated expenditures. Or you could reduce this projected deficiency by eliminating or cutting back on some of your expenses.

Household Budget — Annual

Housing

Mortgage or Rent	_____	Club Membership	_____
Property Taxes	_____	Doctors, Dentists	_____
Insurance	_____	Prescriptions	_____
Utilities	_____	Life Insurance	_____
Repairs	_____	Other Insurance	_____
Food and Household Supplies	_____	Contributions	_____
Clothing	_____	Income Taxes	_____
Transportation		Other Costs	_____
Installment Payments	_____		_____
Insurance	_____	**Total Expenditures**	_____
Fuel	_____		
Maintenance	_____	**Budget Summary:**	
Other Transportation	_____	**Total Household Income**	_____
Phone	_____	**Less Total Expenditures** (from above)	_____
Education	_____		
Entertainment	_____	**Surplus or Deficiency**	_____

Business Budget

You can figure your business budget using the three forms provided on the following pages: the Start-up Expense Projection; the Monthly Expense Projection; and the Cash Flow Projection.

The business budget will be more difficult to establish than your household budget because you have no history to draw on. Nevertheless, make an estimate or best guess of your start-up costs and ongoing monthly expenses. You can verify your assumptions by checking with people in similar businesses, accountants, bankers, or your library.

Start-up Expense Projection

Proceed to fill out the Start-up Expense Projection worksheet on the facing page. On this form, list only those one-time cash outlays you will have to pay in full by the end of your first month in business. If you pay items by installment plan, lease, or loan, show only your first month's payment here.

Consider every detail you will have to put in place to officially start your business operations and list its cost. Will you need to hire an electrician, carpenter, or painter to prepare your working area, or can you do the work yourself for just the cost of the materials? What about installing new or expanded phone service? Will you need a facsimile machine, and if so, can it share a line with your voice phone, or will you use it so frequently that it will need its own designated line? You'll need business cards, and probably stationery for presenting estimates and invoices. How about flyers, brochures, packaging or ads? Will you need materials for manufacturing a product, or will you purchase products to resell?

Business Budget — Start-up* Expense Projection

Fees and Licenses _____

Association Dues _____

Equipment** _____

  Machinery _____

  Fixtures _____

  Furniture _____

  Furnishings _____

  Tools _____

Installation _____

  Telephone _____

  Facsimile _____

  Other _____

Preparation of Working Area _____

  Painting _____

  Carpentry _____

  Electrical _____

  Other _____

Initial Purchases _____

  Business Cards & Stationery _____

  Marketing Brochures _____

  Advertising _____

  Office Supplies _____

  Reference Books _____

  Products for Resale, if any _____

  Materials for Manufacturing, if any _____

Other Expenses _____

_____ _____

Total Start-up Expenses: _____

* These are one-time only costs of starting your business.
** List down-payment only, if not paid in full.

Monthly Expense Projection

Next, fill out the Monthly Expense Projection worksheet on the opposite page. Try to project all expenses that you can think of that will occur as you operate your new business day to day. Add at least ten to fifteen percent extra to each item for contingencies. This is where you will list the amount you'll have to pay each month on any leases or installment payments. It is better to overestimate rather than underestimate your expenses. You do not want to run out of money as you are getting your business off the ground.

Cash Flow Projection

Now that you have estimated your business start-up expenses, and your ongoing monthly expenses, you can combine those with an estimate of your income to see when your business will start making money. Use the Cash Flow Projection worksheet on pages 64 and 65. Estimate all your income for each month and deduct your expenses; the result is your cash flow. If you spend more than you take in, you have a cash deficit or negative cash flow. If you take in more than you spend, you have a cash surplus or positive cash flow.

Unless your start-up costs are very minimal, expect to have a deficit in the early months of your new business. Usually, there will be a gradual build up of cash over time as you attain sales of your product(s) or service(s).

Cash flow is not an absolute as to whether you have a profit or loss in your business, but it sure is a strong indicator of where your business is going. Obviously, you must obtain a positive cash flow if you are to stay in business and grow.

Business Budget — Monthly* Expense Projection

Salaries, if any employees _____

Payroll Taxes, if any employees _____

Telephone _____

Office Supplies _____

Postage _____

Insurance _____

Interest Expense _____

Transportation

   Payments (or lease) _____

   Insurance _____

   Fuel _____

Entertainment _____

Advertising _____

Dues and Subscriptions _____

Shipping and Freight Costs _____

Ongoing Cost of Products for Resale, if any _____

Ongoing Cost of Materials for Manufacturing, if any _____

Other Expenses _____

Total Monthly Expenses Outlay: _____

* For annual costs such as your insurance premium, divide by 12 and list the result as a monthly average.

To complete this form, first write in the amount of your one-time start-up expenses total from page 61 on the line provided for it in the column under month 1. Then, on the next line in the spaces going across for each month write in your monthly expense projection total from page 63.

Next, you will add these two together to fill in the third line in the column for Month 1. Just add your start-up expenses total and your Month 1 expenses to get your first entry in the cumulative expenses line. This sum shows how much you will have paid out to start the business and survive the first month. Now add that figure to your monthly expenses for Month 2, to determine your cumulative expenses through the end of the second month.

Business Budget – Cash Flow Projection

	Month 1	Month 2	Month 3	Month 4	Month 5
Start-up Expenses (from pg. 61)					
Monthly Expenses (from pg. 63)					
Cumulative Expenses For Month 1, add the two lines above; then, add each new month's expenses to your prior total.					
Monthly Income (your best estimate)					
Cumulative Income Here, add each month's income to the total for all prior months to keep a running total.					
Less Cumulative Expenses Repeat your figure from the third line here and subtract it from the line directly above.					
Cash Surplus or Deficit					

Continue adding each new month's expenses to the previous cumulative expense total, to keep a running total of cumulative expenses as you go forward.

For the monthly income line, write in how much income you estimate the business will generate each month. Be conservative, keeping in mind that for the first few months, income may be zero, then gradually increase. Next, for the cumulative income line, add each month's income to the previous cumulative income total to keep a running total.

Finally, subtract your cumulative expense figures (on third line) from your cumulative income figures. When your income is higher than your expenses, you have a cash surplus and probably a profit. When your expenses exceed your income, you have a cash deficit and possibly a loss.

Month 6	Month 7	Month 8	Month 9	Month 10	Month 11	Month 12

Finding Start-up Money

Where do you plan to get the money needed to start up your home business? There are several ways to get this funding. For instance:

- Will it come from your existing salary if you continue to work?
- Will it come from your spouse who will continue working at a full-time job?
- Will it come from your savings?
- Will it come from your family?
- Will it come from friends?
- Will you borrow it from a bank? or
- Will it come from some combination of these?

Whatever method you choose to obtain funding, be sure that the money you will need for both your business and your personal expenses is in place before you start. For initial start-up funds, you may want to investigate the financial assistance programs available through the U.S. Small Business Administration (SBA). For more information, contact the SBA office nearest you or:

U.S. Small Business Administration
(800) 827-5722 (Nationwide)

Your local Small Business Development Center (SBDC) should have financing information available as well. It is also always a good idea to develop a strong relationship with your banker. Your banker, once familiar with your business idea, can be more willing to provide necessary funding.

There is no magic to funding your business. You either have or can get the necessary monies or you can't. Many start-up businesses fail because of inadequate funding; they run out of money before getting to a positive cash flow status. The importance of simplicity, therefore, cannot be overstressed. Take it slow and keep your costs down — you want to succeed and adequate funding is crucial to accomplishing this. For more about financial considerations, see Chapter 6.

Establish Recordkeeping

Opening a business checking account is an important step in starting your new business, because by paying all expenses by check, you have a record of those expenses. By reviewing your checkbook, you will readily see if there are any unreasonable expenditures and can take steps to correct them. If your recordkeeping is to be kept to a minimum, that minimum should be a business checking account. Likewise, as sales of your product(s) or service(s) develops, the payments should be deposited in your new checking account. Here again, this will enable you to have a record of the income of your new business.

A checking account may be all you need for adequate records. An accountant can go through the checkbook each quarter or even once a year to prepare proper financial reports and tax information. In opening a business checking account, investigate and compare the different services and fees provided by several banks. Convenience and a friendly banker should be considered when determining which bank may be right for you. For more information on record keeping, refer to Chapter 7.

Set Up Your Operation

For most businesses you will have to designate an area of your home as an office. Some businesses that produce or distribute a product may require additional space. For your primary work area, choose a space that will be comfortable.

Your Office

The office for your home-based business may be very simple or elaborate depending entirely on the nature of your business, tastes, and pocketbook. For example, if you are selling and delivering baked goods to local stores, your office may simply consist of a desk or dresser drawer where you can keep your checkbook, bills, and receipts. You may not even need a typewriter — handwritten bills which you deliver together with your products may be fine. If, however, customers or clients will be coming to your home, you should try to situate your office in a quiet area and provide a tasteful, professional office setting.

If possible, keep your expenditures for setting up your office low so that you can conserve your capital for other important aspects of your business. You may find that you already have a desk and other suitable furniture that you can use, or you may want to consider inexpensive, used office furniture. You can even make a simple but effective desk by putting a plain, new oak door across two, low file cabinets spaced about 30 inches apart. The back of the file cabinets should be against the wall and the door should be fastened to the wall with screws. This will provide you with both storage and a clear work area. If you feel your business office deems a more elegant, professional setting, consider purchasing new furniture with more interior decor.

When planning your office, consider your needs and don't lose sight of what is essential to get your business going. Make your plans carefully and don't get carried away in spending money on furniture or equipment unless they are a necessary and worthwhile investment.

Office Supplies

With regard to office supplies, again what you will require depends entirely upon your business. You should be able to find everything you need in local office supply stores. Also, companies that sell office supplies through mail-order catalogs are a convenient source and usually offer substantial savings. Use common sense and try to buy in advance only those items you know you will need. Other items can be purchased when the need arises. Remember you can go from clips to copiers to computers as part of your office start up and spend a great deal of money that may not be necessary. So keep it simple and inexpensive.

Business Cards and Stationery

A well-planned business card is a necessity for virtually any home-based business and should be one of your early priorities. You probably also need stationery for correspondence, estimates, and invoices. You may want to use a special logo for your card and also for any business stationery or forms. If you want a custom logo, contact a graphic designer in your area. Be sure to get an estimate of the design cost before you proceed. If you feel you can use a stock logo, check with a local printer or look in mail-order office supply catalogs.

Equipment

The equipment you require will be directly linked to the home-based business you choose. For instance, you will need a computer for a desktop publishing business and may want a packing conveyor for a distribution business. Make sure you clearly separate needs and wants, and initially purchase only needed items. If you ascertain that you need some equipment, look around for low-cost used models or purchase new equipment on an installment plan. Keep your capital expenditures as low as possible.

The usual equipment for an office, such as a computer, facsimile machine, telephone answering machine, and copier, have come down to reasonable prices. Nevertheless, only buy such equipment that you will initially use in the early stages of your start up.

Work Shop Area

Most businesses headquartered from home need office space. Some businesses, however, also need space for production and packing. For example, if you are going to produce and distribute a product from your home, you will need areas for storage and production. If it is at all possible, such areas should be established in the home and not rented. Remember, you want to keep your overhead low; you do not need a rent bill for a small warehouse each month. If you can manage space from a garage, basement, or spare room, it will save you money and be more convenient. There is time to grow into more space once you get your new company up and rolling.

Check Your Insurance

Remember that your business from home most likely will be small, and many types of insurance policies are available to cover many possible occurrences. Having adequate insurance protection and relating it to your small business is important. You should have adequate protection, not excessive protection.

Insurance is similar to many other aspects of a business start up. You want to have enough, but not an overkill. You have to balance coverage with cost.

Check your homeowner's policy to see that you have the proper amounts of coverage to protect the equipment, assets, and risks your home business may have. In most cases, you can add a rider to this policy to also cover your home for business purposes. A rider is an addition to a document, in this case, your insurance policy. For example, if your policy does not specifically cover a home computer, you can often get a rider that does cover computers. This costs a little extra, but provides necessary coverage. Jewelry, furs, silverware, and works of art are usually covered on riders.

An alternative to a rider on your home owner's policy would be to obtain a separate general liability policy to cover your business.

The size and type of home-based business you plan to operate will dictate what insurance coverage is appropriate. Consult an insurance broker or independent agent or a group such as the Home Business Institute to advise you on proper coverage. Check with more than one such provider to compare coverage and costs. Don't allow yourself to be talked into buying more insurance than you really need.

Some types of insurance may be required by law, such as workers' compensation insurance. Keep in mind that if your business will have employees, your legal obligations to have various types of insurance will increase. Make sure to check with your state's insurance department or an agent or broker.

Other types of insurance coverage to consider include:

- Health insurance
- Auto insurance
- Product liability insurance
- Malpractice insurance
- Partnership insurance

An insurance package should meet your start-up needs, fit within your budget, and allow for business growth. For practical advice on how to buy business insurance, understand policies, and lower your costs, take a look at *The Buyer's Guide to Business Insurance*. This book is available at your local book source, library, or from The Oasis Press at (800) 228-2275. This resource helps you determine the types of insurance you need, and shop for the best rates for that coverage. Also the Home Business Institute at 1-888-DIAL-HBI has a insurance consulting desk to advise members.

Create a Sales and Marketing Strategy

Sales are the life blood of any business. Without sales, there is no business no matter how valuable and needed your product(s) or service(s) may be. Sales are essential for continuing operations. To ensure the continuing operation of your new home-based business, you must develop a marketing plan. To begin, ask yourself these questions:

- What is for sale?
- Who are your customers?
- What is your product or service's price?
- What are your selling terms?

At the core of your business are the product(s) or service(s) you will be selling. That's what your new business is all about and why you started in the first place. To identify your customers or clients you must do some research. You may be selling handcrafted mailboxes and find that logical customers for such items are hardware stores. Later, you find that a large home center store might also be a great outlet for your product. You have to do some homework to determine which customers or clients are best for you; where they are; and how they can be reached.

When you determine who they are, you have identified your target market. When you determine where they are, you may want to develop a marketing program to reach them. Consider each of the following points:

- Will you call on them?
- Will you send a flyer?

- Will you put flyers in key locations?
- Will you advertise in newspapers, magazines, etc.?
- Will you use telemarketing?

Much will depend on the amount of money you have allocated for advertising and promoting your product(s) or service(s). Start slowly and build up gradually. This will enable you to keep your costs down while you test different marketing methods. In some cases, word-of-mouth selling from one satisfied customer to another may be all you need.

Small advertising agencies or publicists might be available at a nominal fee to help you with advertising or promotion. But before you get into full-blown marketing and sales, be sure you check out your competition. If you find that you do have competition, what do they offer and at what price? This information should be used to help position your pricing. Of course, there are other factors you should consider when determining your selling price besides competition. Your costs, quality, and design will be important if you are marketing a product. Your presentation, background, and personality might be important in pricing a service.

Lastly, what are your selling terms? Does the customer have to put a deposit down for your product? Is payment due in 30 days? Does your client pay for ten cooking lessons, for example, at the beginning of each session or up-front like school tuition? Will you send invoices? Who pays the freight?

Again, check your competition and try to follow terms that are customary for your type of product(s) or service(s).

Open Your Business and Prepare to Grow

When you have reached this tenth step your new business is off the ground and ready to open. You are in an "operational mode." You want to make sure at this point that your business grows and becomes a success. To succeed, you need to:

- Plan your growth.
- Know your costs.
- Grow slowly.
- Keep quality high.
- Service your clients.
- Get feedback from customers.

One of the best ways to grow is to have satisfied customers. Customers are the best judge of how well you are delivering your product(s) or service(s) to the market. If they are satisfied, you are doing things right. Try to get as much feedback as you can so you can fine-tune your new business and continue on a slow and steady path towards growth and success.

Stay in touch with your customers, and let them know you appreciate their business. A good way to do this is by sending business-to-business communications as a quick and inexpensive method to build customer and client relations. This can be done by letter or by using cards.

To start to address the future of your business, map out a simple plan spelling out in writing the steps you will take to get more clients or customers for your product(s) or service(s), as well as the steps you will take to properly supply increased quantities of product(s) or service(s) to your growing company. And, lastly, describe how you plan to keep this growth steadily supplied with funding and people power.

Mile Post

By completing these ten start-up steps for your home business, you are well on your way to learning what it takes to be your own boss. Remember to keep your costs and objectives within sight and to plan for your business' future growth carefully.

Chapter
5

Service and Product Businesses

Businesses operated from the home can be defined in terms of two distinct categories: those that offer a service and those that offer a product. Product businesses may offer some services as part of their business, but do not confuse these with service businesses.

Service businesses operated from the home, once placing second to product businesses, are mushrooming to account for the majority of home-based businesses today. These businesses include services performed in the home, such as small day care centers, desktop publishing operations, and cooking classes; and those services performed outside the home, such as lawn care, dog walking, and house sitting.

Product businesses can be divided into two subcategories:

- Businesses in which the manufacturer or creator of the product is also the marketer; and
- Businesses in which the product offered has been manufactured by others.

In either case, the product or products in question must be distributed. There are many methods of product distribution and fulfillment, including distributorships, franchising, and mail order, all of which are discussed later in this chapter.

This chapter focuses on the differences between service and product businesses and discusses some of the opportunities available for each type of business.

Service Businesses

A service business provides a service to its clients or customers. While this definition sounds very straightforward, the kinds of services that can be offered by a home-based service business range from the simple to the complex, and depend on the skills, talents, interests, and education of the service provider.

Types of Service Business

The following list of service businesses outlines some of the areas in which people have chosen to operate service enterprises. Note that depending on your particular strengths, there are certain service areas that may be more suited to you than others.

- Business services advertising — mailing list maintenance, and resumé and letter writing.
- Child services — babysitting, small day care centers and children's party planning.
- Computer services — hardware, software, repair, installation, training, and tutoring.
- Consulting services — business, marketing, and engineering.
- Desktop publishing — typesetting, book and manuscript preparation, signs, pamphlets and advertising materials.
- Education services — tutoring and language training.
- Food businesses — catering and cooking classes.
- Home services — house watching, plant watering, lawn care, pet care, food shopping for the house-bound, and house cleaning.
- Service registries — nurse registry, nanny registry, babysitting registry.

The list can go on and on and continues to grow as more people become involved in home-based service businesses.

Where to Conduct Business

Decide whether you want your customers to come to your home or whether you want to take your service to them. Of course, just by their definition, some services require that you go outside your home, such as lawn care or housesitting, while others are more suited to operation within your home, such as a small day care center. Other businesses, such as tax consulting or finance businesses, can be done in either place, in which case, the question is: Your place or their place? Whatever service business you choose, when dealing with your clients or customers, you should determine whether the service will be offered in your home, outside your home, or both.

Your Place

Certain businesses require clients to actually enter your home, such as guests at your bed and breakfast inn or cooking classes in your kitchen. For these businesses, you need to give special attention to the availability of space and family scheduling. It would never do to have your teenage son and his friends raiding the refrigerator while you are trying to demonstrate the proper techniques for filling puff pastries; or late-night sibling battles while your bed and breakfast guests are trying to get a good night's sleep. A professional atmosphere is important if you want to create a businesslike environment for your visiting clients.

> Diane, an accomplished cook specializing in Chinese food, was faced with the problems of creating a professional environment for her clients when she decided to set up cooking classes in her home kitchen. Beginning originally as a cooking instructor in a local high school adult education program, Diane decided that she could make better money and have more freedom if she took her talent into her home and invited students to work with her there. Being accustomed to the privacy of the high school home economics kitchen, Diane was not prepared for the conflicts that she was to encounter.

The major problem was scheduling. With four growing children and a medium-sized house, it was not easy to operate a class while the television was on in the next room and children needed help with their homework. She decided to schedule her cooking classes during the morning and afternoon hours when her children were at school. While this solved the problem of creating a professional atmosphere, because Diane could focus all her attention on her students, it did not address the fact that most of Diane's potential clients preferred evening and Saturday classes.

To alleviate the problem, Diane called a family meeting during which she explained her dilemma. With a bit of give and take on both sides, Diane was able to work out a schedule that satisfied both the needs of her clients and her family. She now conducts most of her classes on Saturday mornings and two evenings during the week.

Diane was able to solve her scheduling problems because she had the support of her family. This is very important if you plan to bring a service business into your home. Before you start, seriously consider the space you have available and the times when you can give one hundred percent attention to the services you are providing.

The Customer's Place

For service businesses where the service is provided at your customer's home, considerations are different. While you must maintain your paperwork and a telephone answering machine at your home office, most of the work is done in your clients' homes, offices, or work spaces. Babysitting, dog walking, pet feeding and grooming, plant watering, housesitting, food shopping, catering, and gardening are examples of home service businesses.

While a professional appearance and attitude are important for these ventures, your home office can be more relaxed because you will not be bringing clients into the family environment.

> One example of a home service businesswoman is Julie, a 60-year-old widow. Julie wanted to earn some extra money, and while she didn't want to hold down a traditional full-time or part-time job, she did want something that would get her out of the house. As a lover of animals, particularly cats, Julie was a natural for a pet-feeding service. To initiate her new venture, Julie prepared a professional-looking flyer that announced her home service business. She also made visits to local veterinary offices and hospitals where she left her name and a few flyers to be given to prospective clients. To keep an air of professionalism, Julie set up a separate telephone line for her business with an answering machine attached to it. This way, she was able to screen her messages before calling potential clients to set up an interview.

> While Julie's business is run out of her home, it does not affect the daily routine of household activities. By taping phone messages on a machine, Julie is able to call back potential clients at her convenience. Julie feels this helps to create customer confidence and attributes much of her success to her businesslike methods.

When entering a client's home or office to perform a service, remember to act in a businesslike manner and focus on the job at hand. It may be fun to socialize, but the client is paying for your service and has in some way adjusted his or her routine to allow you time to do your work. If your service requires physical activity, this is no excuse to dress in a sloppy manner. When you are out in the field, maintain a professional appearance and attitude at all times.

Service Franchises

Whether you decide to perform your service in or outside your home, you may be uncertain about starting your own business from the ground up. If this is the case, you might be interested in a service franchise, where some of the start-up process may already be done.

A franchise is a legal agreement by which, you, the franchisee, purchase the right to promote and distribute a service or product using the corporate name of the franchisor or parent company. Traditionally, franchises have helped would-be business owners bring down the initial costs of starting a business and shorten the amount of time necessary to get the business started, therefore, increasing the chances of success. These factors — combined with the lower costs of operating a home-based business and the freer lifestyle it offers — are making home-based franchises more popular than ever.

As more women enter the work force and as the percentage of two-income households increases, time becomes a more valuable commodity and people seek to spend their free time pursuing recreational activities. Service businesses that contribute to increasing free time are becoming more popular. Some franchise opportunities available to meet this demand for more free time include babysitting services and registries, and home maintenance and cleaning services. Another form of business that has recently developed in this area is the mobile franchise. These businesses operate out of cars, vans, or trucks and deliver services right to their clients' doorstep. Popular services offered by mobile franchises include carpet, upholstery, and home cleaning, car washing, and interior and exterior house painting.

The growth of entrepreneurship has also increased the need for various business services, and franchise opportunities geared to these entrepreneurs — such as computer, financial, advertising, telephone answering and word-processing services — are increasing in number.

The advantages of entering into a service franchise are obvious. You are given the benefit of the parent company's experience and help in marketing, promotional, and recordkeeping techniques. In some cases, the franchisor will offer courses in marketing and distribution to help you get started, but you must operate according to the franchisor's procedures.

Investing in Your Service Business

Whether you perform a service in your home or on the outside, and whether you start your own business or enter into a franchise agreement, there will be an initial investment for the start-up of your service company. If equipment is necessary you will need capital for its purchase. Supplies and stationery may be needed to get started. Fees to lawyers, accountants, list brokers, and franchisors should be analyzed. Marketing and advertising costs are another consideration. If you enter into a franchise, chances are that the parent company has an advertising program in effect that will help to attract customers to your door.

If you are on your own, you will have to do your own advertising. If your service is performed in a local area, marketing costs can be kept to a minimum. Print one-page flyers and post them in appropriate public gathering places. Ads in local newspapers and publications are another way to attract customers to your service. In all cases, the investment in your new business should be kept to a minimum, commensurate with getting the business off the ground properly. See Chapter 4 for more information on how to estimate your investment.

Product Businesses

Product businesses are concerned with the manufacture and sale of a product or products. As defined earlier, product businesses include:

- Businesses in which the manufacturer or creator of the product is also the marketer; and
- Businesses in which the merchandise offered has been manufactured by someone else.

The common factor in both cases is that every product requires a distribution system, and this becomes a major part of all product businesses. Before learning about the different methods of product distribution, however, first consider some of the differences between product businesses and the considerations that must be made by the owners of each of these businesses.

Creator as Marketer

In independent ventures, in which the creator of the product is also the marketer, marketing and distribution as well as production must be considered. Businesses most often falling into this category include those in which a hobby or craft item is being sold. Food specialties and baked goods are also popular creator-marketer products as are novelty and personalized items.

> Take Frank McNamara, for example, a middle-aged husband and father who has a keen interest in family heraldry and history. Always interested in his family's Irish roots, Frank did some research into his family's background and discovered that they had an interesting-looking family crest. Being a talented artist, Frank drew his own version of the design a stylized lion and created a shield-shaped plaque on which to mount it.
>
> It wasn't too long until all the McNamaras in Frank's family wanted their own plaques. This gave Frank an idea — if the members of his family were so enthusiastic about his plaque, then possibly McNamaras located around the country would also want it.
>
> First, Frank did a search to learn if anyone else was producing a similar product. When he found that he had very little competition, Frank

decided to proceed with the project and developed a method for mass-producing the designs he mounted on plaques. Frank then completed several plaques, which he stored in his basement workshop. Deciding that the best way to reach customers was through the U.S. Postal Service, Frank purchased a list of McNamaras with their addresses. He took a photograph of one of his finished plaques and had this reproduced in a brochure that included a brief McNamara family history along with ordering information. When orders began coming in, Frank shipped out the plaques at a reduced mail-order rate he had arranged through his local post office.

Frank had done his homework well. As the manufacturer and distributor of his own product, he had followed these simple steps to success:

- Determine if your product has a market.
- Locate other companies selling similar products.

Often, people involved in these product businesses like Frank McNamara, have been involved with the product they sell for quite some time. If you initiate and design your own product line, consider the initial investments required for the purchase of raw materials and tools and how the product will be sold at craft fairs, via mail-order, or on consignment in local shops. Often overlooked are market research aspects, advertising, and the best method of distribution. Consider the following points to ensure your business success:

- Choose a method to advertise your product.
- Choose a method to distribute your product.

If you are considering manufacturing your own product, don't neglect the importance of market research and advertising. Depending on the method of advertising you choose — direct mail, classified or display ads in newspapers and magazines, flyers, or displays in local storefront windows — some investment will be necessary, and you should do your homework to determine which method will best attract the customers you want.

Packaging is another aspect of marketing which is important for creating an attractive presentation of your product. While the cost and type of packaging will vary, it should be considered as part of your initial product investment.

Don't forget your method of product delivery. How you get your product into the hands of your customers is almost as important as creating the product itself. You may chose to ship your merchandise through the mail or via other carriers. If you prefer to sell directly to your customers, you can set up a small shop in your home (check local zoning regulations first), or you can rent booth space at local craft and gift fairs. Another method is to place your product on the shelves of local retail and specialty shops. You can begin by placing your product with shop owners on consignment. They pay you only for product that has been sold. As your product's popularity increases, try selling larger quantities to store owners and request payment on delivery or within ten days.

Marketer of Products Created by Others

Businesses from home that resell products manufactured by others focus primarily on the marketing and distribution of those products. Home business owners who produce and sell a product and those who resell products manufactured by others have somewhat different considerations as to why they choose a particular product. Nevertheless, certain factors apply to both. Most people do better at selling products they are familiar with or that they enjoy working with. A retired history teacher, for example, may not be comfortable selling machine parts, just as a machinist may not be happy selling reference books and encyclopedias. Lack of knowledge about a product and its use will surely affect sales.

Home-based product businesses that fall into this category include distributorships and product franchises.

Distributorships

Not to be confused with distribution, a distributorship is a business in which you, the owner, obtain rights from a manufacturer to dispense its product or products. The amount of responsibility taken on by the distributorship for marketing, warehousing, and product distribution will vary depending on the arrangement.

Distribution requirements for distributorships are the same as those for the business owner who has created his or her own product. The difference is that in a distributorship, the product is made by someone else.

In most cases, you must purchase up front and warehouse the product you intend to sell. This requires an initial investment for the purchase (at wholesale prices) of product that will be inventoried. The amount of storage space needed must also be considered with thought to how much inventory should be acquired.

People who choose to operate product distribution companies usually prefer to stay at home and ship materials out of some room or garage. Others may be happier selling door to door. As you read the following descriptions of distribution systems, keep in mind your strengths that could be applied to helping you develop a successful business.

Exclusive Distribution Rights. In cases where you actively seek a distributorship from a manufacturer, the chances of obtaining exclusive distribution rights in a particular region are the greatest. This means that the manufacturer has agreed to allow you the opportunity to set up a marketing and product distribution operation in an area in which it has promised not to make the same arrangement with anyone else. Usually, you must prove your ability to:

- Establish a customer base.
- Deal with competition.
- Form an advertising and promotional plan.
- Handle distribution.

There are many opportunities for obtaining an exclusive distribution arrangement. The key is your ability to identify a product that you can market and sell. Perhaps there is a product you can distribute that is related to one of your hobbies. Or maybe there is a product sold only outside the United States. Many foreign companies are seeking distributors in the United States to handle their products. Look through foreign magazines, or if you are lucky enough to travel, look for products that you think would sell well in the American market. This will require some research, but it will be well worth it to gain sole distributorship rights to a product that you help make popular in the United States. For a good example of exclusive distribution rights, refer to "International Distributorship" in Chapter 1.

Local Distributors and Manufacturer's Representatives. To keep their overhead low, many manufacturers seek to sell their products in local areas. Look for advertisements for distributorships or manufacturer's representatives offered by such companies in entrepreneurial and small business publications. For a list of general business publications, see Appendix B.

In these arrangements, the manufacturer of the product will probably already have completed most of the research required to determine potential customers, existing competition, means of advertising, and method of distribution. What the manufacturer is looking for is someone to warehouse its product and distribute the product in a local area. If you need help with the required initial investment, low-interest financing arrangements are often made available.

Brochures, marketing plans, types of customers to approach, and free samples are supplied to you. Depending on the arrangement, you purchase the product up front and warehouse it.

You then go about establishing a client base by either selling door to door in residential areas or retail outlets; or by placing advertisements in local publications and then fulfilling orders; or taking orders which are sent back to the manufacturer for fulfillment.

If a product is a one-time sell, as are most appliances, encyclopedias, or any product the consumer uses over and over again, your distributorship has established a base for future sales. If the product is consumable, as are baked goods, food specialties, and items sold in vending machines, then your distributorship has established a base of customers for repeat sales.

Rackjobbers. As a rackjobber, you purchase and warehouse products from manu-facturers and wholesalers, which you then resell to retail outlets, including drug-stores, variety stores, and grocery stores, filling shelves as the product moves. Part of the rackjobbing arrangement is the placement in these stores of racks and point-of-purchase (POP) displays supplied by the manufacturer. You load these racks with a set quantity of prepackaged merchandise. The racks may have sev-eral different items or just one. In each case, these point-of-purchase items are packaged so that customers walking through a store will want to pick them off the racks and drop them into their shopping carts. They are "silent salespeople."

If you are a rackjobber, you go around to retail outlets asking for space to place these racks and POP displays. In most cases, the retailer takes the product on con-signment, meaning that it pays only for those items that are sold.

You periodically check the racks and restock the items sold. You then bill the retailer for what was sold. Not having to pay for merchandise until it sells is an excellent point for convincing store owners to take racks into their stores. If the manufacturer has run a marketing campaign for the products available on the racks, consumers will already be aware of their availability and will ask for the products. If a product is already in demand, the retailer will want it, and your job is made much easier.

Wagonjobbers. Wagonjobbers are smaller versions of their cousin, the rackjobber. These distributorship ventures operate out of cars, vans, and trucks. Often offered as franchise opportunities, these businesses provide door-to-door sales and prod-uct delivery. Usually operated as a residential distribution arrangement in which the product is delivered directly to the home, these businesses will also sell to small retail and service enterprises.

For example, you may represent a beauty supply company. Going to various beauty salons in a local area, you would drop off samples of a new shampoo and conditioning product and return in a few days to see if the product has made a hit. If it has, then you stock the salon with the product which is stored in your car. This efficient method of distribution allows for taking orders and delivery of product at the same time.

Shopping Parties. Other distributorship arrangements can be operated on a smaller scale, and you can sell products by sponsoring home shopping parties.

Some manufacturers prepare catalogs with fixed prices of the items they offer. These items are not usually available in retail outlets but may be sold through independent dealers at home shopping parties. Such products include Tupperware®, lingerie, diet and food products, household goods, holiday greeting cards, and candy. You would take all orders, store the items when the shipment arrives, collect all monies, and deliver the product to customers. Paperwork and recordkeeping are usually handled by the parent company, where commission amounts are calculated and paid out.

Multilevel Marketing. Multilevel marketing involves not only the sale and distribution of product, but the development of a "downline" or increasing levels of dealerships as well. In most multilevel marketing arrangements, an umbrella company provides a product line that is distributed through home-based dealerships.

As a dealer, you are free to sell door to door, via parties and meetings you hold in your home, or by any other direct sales method. While the sale of product is the main goal of these arrangements, the acquisition of new dealerships is also a primary focus, and the parent company supplies you with rudimentary sales materials aimed at enticing new dealers to enter into the multilevel arrangement. Your incentive is the commission that increases as more and more dealerships are developed within your region. For each dealer added, a percentage of the commission is fed back to you and so the commission is broken down through the many levels. The more dealers there are at each level, the better it is for the dealers that are at the higher levels in this multilevel marketing system.

An investment in large quantities of product may be required for new dealers entering into these schemes. Research the company offering a multilevel arrangement before you release any of your money. You don't want to end up with a lot of product and no where to sell it because the market in your region has already been saturated by other dealers hoping to make the same "killing."

Product Franchises

As with the service franchise, marketing and distribution materials are supplied to you by the parent company and you benefit from their experience with promotional and recordkeeping techniques.

While there are many more home-based service franchises than product franchises, a franchise business is worth looking into if you are interested in pursuing a distribution business, but feel you need the support of a parent company to help you get started.

Home-based product franchises are available in these areas: children's products, health and beauty products, special occasion goods, print products (magazines, newsletters, newspapers, books), photographic products, and other miscellaneous arts and crafts products.

Mail Order

Mail order is fast becoming one of the most popular businesses from home and is a good example of a business that is able to market a product in several ways:

- Creator as marketer;
- Marketer of product created by others; or
- Marketing your own or purchased products, or both.

Whichever way you choose to go, first search out items that are not usually sold in retail outlets. There are many items to choose from for your mail-order distributor business. These include novelty and personalized items, gifts, and hobby/home/business items. The list could be endless.

Do your homework and find a market that will buy your product before you make an initial investment. It also helps to determine who your competition will be so you can create alternative marketing campaigns to bring attention to your products' special qualities. Try to find a niche market or special twist that makes your line of products different from all the others.

Mailing lists can be purchased from established companies selling to a market similar to the one you want to reach. Or, you can work with a list broker. These are often advertised in the small business and entrepreneurial magazines found in your local stationery store or bookstore. Expect to make an initial investment to cover the cost of your product, advertising, promotion, and shipping. Because you will need to warehouse the product you intend to sell, give some attention to storage space.

If you do plan to start a home-based mail-order business, learn to write marketing copy and invest in colorful and attractive literature. If you feel this is beyond your capabilities, obtain the services of a small advertising agency. Mail-order promotions and catalogs are being received by your potential customers at an increasing rate as more and more businesses hop on the mail-order business wagon. The importance of making your products stand out as special and different from the rest cannot be overemphasized.

Your Best Interests Come First

No matter what type of home-based business you choose, one theme prevails — there are no sure bets. It takes work and persistence to develop your own independent product or service company. Do your homework first. Research the product or service and, when necessary, the company offering it. Ask these questions.

- Do you feel comfortable promoting this product or service?
- Do you have any expertise in the area that can help with marketing strategies?

- Are you an experienced enough marketer to take on a distribution business that requires heavy sales work?

- Do you have enough room in your house or garage to warehouse a product? If you do, how many months worth of supply can you manage?

- Do you have the facilities to create and maintain accurate inventory and sales records?

Before making an investment to distribute a product or offer a service in any area, check the fine print. Are you being offered sole rights to a region, or will you be competing with other distributors and dealers? Get information about market penetration and avoid distributing a product that has already reached saturation in your area.

Don't get caught just being a large order for a marketer who tries to get you hooked into a business with a large, up-front investment. Check your options, and make sure you can return any unsold goods.

Marketing Tips

Remember that distributorships, franchises, multilevel marketing arrangements, and sometimes mail-order operations are part of marketing plans originated by larger corporations to keep their overhead and operating costs down. They have already produced the merchandise or developed the service, what they are looking for are marketing representatives and distribution outlets.

If you are unsure about your marketing and advertising abilities, take the time and money to invest in a course or two or obtain the services of a small advertising agency. Books and magazines are also available to give you advice on how to write a good direct-mail piece or letter.

Learn how to analyze mailing lists and operate a test to determine which lists work best for you. Get help in writing classified or larger display ads for magazines and newspapers and learn how to put a brochure or flyer together. Keep in mind that personally placing your flyers and brochures in or on mailboxes is illegal; however, you can place your advertisements on car windshields and store bulletin boards. Look into cable television or radio advertising. Put your name in with the local stores in your area and put your card or flyer on bulletin boards in corporate office buildings, libraries, or government offices.

Mile Post

There is no limit to the ways in which you can get the word out about your new product or service. So, get out there and pursue it!

Chapter
6

Legal, Regulatory, and Financial Considerations

Legal Issues

A range of laws and regulations will affect the way in which you operate your home-based business. The ones that affect your business will depend, in large part, upon the state in which you operate your business and the type of business you select. Certain federal laws and rules — such as the federal tax laws — will also apply. Understanding applicable rules not only saves you unwanted complications and problems, it also provides you and your business with substantial benefits, such as:

• Saving on income taxes;

- Avoiding unnecessary permits and license fees and filings; and
- Being more confident when dealing with customers or clients.

In the early stages, it may be useful to talk informally with a friend who is a lawyer. Because of the variety and complexity of many laws and regulations, attempting to advise yourself on legal matters can be a mistake; even good lawyers tend to avoid representing themselves. This does not mean that you need to hire a major law firm to draft complex documents. If you can use your entrepreneurial talents to obtain some initial, basic legal advice and guidance at little or no cost, you will have acquired a significant asset for your business.

The variety of laws and regulations that could affect your home business make it difficult to write a comprehensive guide to legal issues for home-based businesses. This chapter does not and cannot give you all the answers. Rather, it will introduce you to a series of basic legal issues that you will most likely confront.

Ideally, this chapter will help you ask your lawyer important and useful questions which should improve the value and quality of the legal advice you receive.

Your objective is to use the law as an ally, not to consider it as a foe. Proper legal decisions can protect you and your business, provide legitimate economic benefits, and minimize distractions from the important tasks of serving customers and managing a successful operation. In general, careful attention at the outset will save you from having to spend a great amount of time and money to correct any future problems.

Legal Forms of Business Organization

One of the first decisions you must make when starting your new business is to choose which legal form of business organization you will adopt. There are four basic forms: the sole proprietorship, the partnership, the corporation, and the limited liability company. Regardless of which legal form you choose, the laws of your state will have a significant effect on its costs and benefits. Although an organizational choice often can be changed, making a good initial choice can save you time, money, and trouble. In addition to the discussion of legal forms in Chapter 4, read the following general observations on each of the four legal forms of business organization, and consult with your attorney before making any final decisions.

Sole Proprietorship

A sole proprietorship is the easiest form of business organization to adopt for an individual owner/operator. In effect, you are the organization. Basic characteristics include:

- **Unlimited personal liability.** Your personal assets may be at risk to cover business liabilities.

- **No separate legal entity.** Ownership interests cannot be given out easily, which may limit options for attracting investors.

- **Few legal formalities.** A simple state filing for a fictitious business name may be all that is required.

- **No special laws.** Most states do not have legal regulations governing sole proprietorships.

- **Cumbersome transfers.** There is no organization to be transferred; therefore, assets and liabilities must be transferred themselves.

- **No separation of ownership and management.** You are both the owner and the operator.

Partnership

A partnership can be simple or complex. This organizational form is appropriate when there is more than one owner. Because more than one owner is involved, a written agreement among the partners is desirable, although in the case of a general partnership, it usually is not required by law. A partnership agreement, if it is comprehensive, can be costly — sometimes more costly than the documents needed to form a corporation.

A general partnership has at least two partners who each have full managerial control and unlimited personal liability, unless there is an agreement to the contrary.

A limited partnership has at least one general and one limited partner. Like a corporation, a written document is required to form a limited partnership; it defines the partners' roles. Typically, a general partner has managerial control and unlimited personal liability. A limited partner has little or no involvement in management and liability limited to the value of his or her ownership interest. It is unlikely that your home-based business would need to use the relatively complex limited partnership form of organization — particularly in its early stages. Basic characteristics for either type of partnership include:

- **Limited liability.** Ordinarily, limited partners in a limited partnership are not personally liable for partnership debts and liabilities.

- **Unlimited liability**. General partners in a general partnership are fully liable for partnership debts and liabilities.

- **Limited transferability of interests.** General partnership interests ordinarily cannot be transferred easily. Limited partnership interests, however, can be transferred in certain circumstances. Limited partnership interests may be desirable for investors who do not want a managerial role.

- **Several legal formalities and special laws.** Like corporate directors and officers, limited partnerships have a fiduciary duty to their partners.

- **No separate taxable entity.** A general or limited partnership does not pay a separate tax on income, provided that it is formed and operated in accordance with special laws and regulations that define a partnership for tax purposes. This avoids the double taxation which affects corporations.

Corporation

A corporation is the most complex and formal type of business organization, making it costly; however, it will tend to offer substantial flexibility in arranging ownership, financing, control, and limitation of liability, among other things. Special types of corporations, such professional and nonprofit corporations, are not discussed here. Required corporate formalities may make incorporating cumbersome for your small and beginning businesses. Be sure to get advice from your attorney or professional adviser before you incorporate. Basic corporate characteristics include:

- **Limited personal liability.** In general, you will be liable for corporate debts only to the extent of your investment in the corporation.

- **Separate legal entity.** Ownership and management may be combined or separated. Stock can be sold to investors or pledged as collateral, creating options for obtaining outside financing.

- **Legal formalities.** A corporation exists only after necessary documents are filed with state authorities. State laws affect many aspects of a corporation's behavior. Alternative: Some state laws recognize a close corporation, which is owned by a small number or people. This option, if available to you, may reduce the complexities and costs of formation and operation.

- **An independent "legal person."** A corporation pays taxes, enters into contracts, incurs liabilities, and sues and is sued. It acts through its officers who are authorized to act for the corporation.

- **Options for control.** Typically, stockholders vote and have ultimate control over a corporation. Directors have overall responsibility for directing the corporation, in accordance with the wishes of the stockholders who elect them. Officers are elected by the directors and make day-to-day decisions in accordance with the general policies of the directors.

A potential disadvantage of a corporation is the double taxation of its income that is distributed to its shareholders. If a corporation has taxable income, pays corporate income taxes on it, and the shareholders withdraw money in the form of a dividend, they will also pay tax on the dividend, as a rule. Thus, the use of a corporation can obviously be disadvantageous if it results in this double taxation of the business' income. With good tax planning, however, most incorporated small businesses can avoid double taxation.

In some circumstances, it may be useful to organize an S corporation, which does not pay a separate corporate-level tax. The first thing to understand clearly about S corporations (formerly referred to as Subchapter S corporations) is that they are no different than any other corporation under state law in terms of corporate law requirements, limited liability of shareholders, or any other aspect except tax treatment. In fact, some states do not even recognize S corporation elections for tax purposes. An S corporation is simply a regular corporation that meets certain requirements and which has to be treated somewhat like a partnership for federal tax purposes.

Subchapter S election maybe an attractive alternative for small companies. A sub-chapter S corporation allows profits or losses to go directly to the shareholders; the possibility of double federal taxation is virtually eliminated. State tax laws vary and should be checked when choosing a Subchapter S election for your corporation. Shareholders include their portion of the company's profits or losses as part of their gross income and are taxed at their individual rates. The S corporation does not pay any taxes on profits.

An S corporation must:

- Have no more than 75 shareholders;
- Have no nonresident alien stockholder;
- Issue only one class of stock;
- Be a domestic corporation, meaning it is incorporated in the state where it is located; and
- Not be a member of an affiliated group.

Limited Liability Companies and Limited Liability Partnerships

Starting with the state of Wyoming in 1977 and ending with the Hawaii legislature in 1996, every state has now passed laws creating a new type of legal entity called a "limited liability company" (or LLC). In addition, all states except Wyoming have now adopted a similar type of entity, the limited liability partnership (or LLP). The LLP is quite similar to an LLC except it may be operated like a regular partnership.

These new entities which resemble (and are taxed as) partnerships offer limited liability, like corporations.

At this point, it would make good sense for almost any sole proprietor to become an LLC since the IRS will treat their income as being that of a sole proprietor. In short, you gain the benefits of limited liability for your sole proprietorship without any increase in your federal tax compliance chores.

Indeed, it may soon become standard practice for any form of business, including sole proprietorships, partnerships, or corporations to create LLCs for new business ventures.

This new form of business is in place in all 50 states. The IRS has passed rules that apply to this new form of business organization.

Prudent advice from a knowledgeable lawyer, in choosing the right business form for your new business can benefit you greatly in the long run.

Legal Start-up Considerations

Regardless of the form of business organization you select, there are a series of legal-related, start-up issues that affect virtually every business. They include organizational documents, ownership interest, valuation and capitalization, and agreements among owners.

Organizational Documents

One of the first things you need to investigate when starting your business is to see whether or not you need to file any organizational documents. Depending on your legal form of business organization, required organizational documents may include articles of incorporation, a certificate of limited partnership, a partnership agreement, a fictitious business name statement, or a state business license.

Legal documents should cover who will control the organization, which is one of the most important aspects of any business. A definition of the business' purpose also helps the owners focus on the business' goals. The relationship among owners and how additional owners are admitted to the business are also important points to cover.

After the organizational documents and regulations have been addressed, you must then tackle the ownership interest issue.

Ownership Interest

If you are considering a corporation or partnership, you will need to make some decisions on how ownership interest will be set up in your business.

If you are using corporate stock, your corporation will have to spell out what voting rights that stock carries and address such issues as will there be dividends rights or not.

If you are going to operate a partnership, then a determination should be made early on as to the distribution of income and gains that should be made to each partner. Other important questions must be answered, such as:

- Will partners receive income in accordance with their contributions to the partnership?
- Will all partners have to contribute money to the partnership in exchange for partnership shares?

There are many possibilities, subject to various tax limitations. A lawyer's advice on the allocation and distribution of partnership income is important. After you have determined what the interests are in your corporation or partnership and what goes with that ownership, attach a value to that ownership interest.

Valuation and Capitalization

At the start, what is an ownership interest in the business worth? Initial decisions may affect the price at which you can sell additional interest to later investors. A cheap sale at the start may limit your business' value in its early stages. Yet, it is typical for initial owners of a business with few assets to acquire their ownership interests at a minimal cost.

If you acquire an ownership interest for less than "fair value" or in exchange for providing services to the business, you may realize taxable income. Make sure you do not leave yourself open to this liability without having the necessary funds to pay such taxes.

State laws may not permit some forms of payment. For example, a promise of future services to the business may not be legal payment for an ownership interest.

Have you abided by any state or federal rules that require certain minimum contributions of money from owners? For example, the general partner of a limited partnership typically must provide at least 1% of the partnership's capital.

Agreements Among Owners

Even if not required, legal agreements among owners are often prudent and desirable, and should be considered.

For instance, when dealing with your corporate or partnership start up, consider some of the following questions as important aspects of any legal agreement:

- Can one owner freely admit an additional owner, even if the other existing owners do not want or like the new person? How will this be spelled out?
- What happens to the business if an owner dies or wants to get out?
- What happens to the ownership interest of a dead or departed owner?
- Should the owners agree to a specific control arrangement, such as electing a board of directors, that reflects the interests or each of the owners?
- What benefits will the business provide to an owner's family?

Good stockholder and partnership agreements can address these issues so they do not become bones of contention at a later date.

Regulatory Issues

Different states and different businesses present varying regulatory considerations. Some types of business, particularly those that may affect the environment, can be subject to complex and extensive regulation. Although most home-based businesses are not likely to be heavily regulated, there are some basic regulatory considerations you need to address. They include:

- **Permission to do business.** Most states require a license to do business. Even a sole proprietorship may have to make this simple filing. To find out which state agency to contact regarding licensing requirements for your business, contact your secretary of state's office or one-stop permit center, if available. Be aware that city and county governments also may have their own licensing requirements.

- **Tax reporting.** A federal tax identification number must be obtained for your business. This number is used when filing necessary city, county, state, or federal tax returns for your business. A separate state number may be required for filing specific state items, such as sales tax and unemployment insurance.

- **Fictitious business names.** Most states require that any business name — other than that of the owner's true name — be registered with its secretary of state's office. This registration prevents other companies from using your business name.

- **Patents, trademarks, and service marks.** You should register any of these items to protect them from infringement.

- **Zoning laws.** Check to see if there are any zoning laws in your area that apply to any activities you will conduct in your home.

Financial Issues

When starting your business, you may not have sufficient funds to cover the basic costs. To determine if you have sufficient funds, you need to first calculate what your basic costs really are. Your exercises on estimating your investment in Chapter 4 should help you do this calculation.

Sources of Financing

The options for satisfying your required business start-up needs will depend upon many factors, including personal savings, ownership of other assets, and the interest and available capital of friends and potential partners. To obtain capital from outside sources is likely to be the single greatest obstacle to starting up your business. If you do not have sufficient funds on hand to capitalize your business entirely on your own, you will have little choice but to seek outside contributions. What will investors get in return?

Banks

If you obtain money from a bank, the bank will want you to pay interest, probably to guarantee repayment of borrowed funds personally, and perhaps to pledge a personal asset (such as your home) as collateral. Can you afford the costs of bank financing? Are you willing to risk personal assets? Even if you are prepared to assume the risks and burdens, you may not be able to locate a bank that will loan money for your fledgling business on terms that you consider reasonable.

Family and Friends

You may be able to find friends or family members who will loan you money for your business. Like a bank, they probably will want interest payments and, perhaps, some guarantee of repayment, such as a personal commitment. A friend or family member, however, is likely to be more flexible than a bank. Transactions with family members may raise special tax considerations that should be examined.

Outside Investors

Another option is to seek outside equity investors — people who will purchase an ownership interest in your business. Creditors, such as a bank, have a right to certain payments, but they do not have an ownership interest in your business. A problem is that start-up equity capital is likely to be expensive — if it can be obtained at all. An equity investor is likely to ask for a substantial ownership interest in your business. What degree of control are you willing to sell?

Keep in mind that although you may be able to involved with an equity investor, it is unlikely in the early stages of a home business, that you could attract such an investor.

Tax and Legal Aspects

In addition to availability of capital, tax considerations can affect whether you seek debt or equity investors. For example, interest payments on debt are a deductible business expense, but dividend payments on corporate stock generally are not deductible.

Whether you seek equity or debt investors, you will face significant legal considerations because of state and federal laws that affect the sale of securities. A security can take many forms, and it certainly includes stock, limited partnership interests, and most common debt obligations. If someone is investing money in your business and is relying on your skills — or the skills of your active partners and managers — to produce value for him or her, he or she almost certainly will have acquired a security from you.

Elaborate federal and state laws have been adopted to protect purchasers of securities from being deceived and to ensure that decisions to buy securities are made on an informed basis. These federal and state securities laws are complex and varied and may require certain filings. They almost certainly will restrict what you can say and whom you can solicit. If you are going to solicit outside investors, consult a lawyer's assistance.

Many small businesses are quite casual about the way in which they solicit investors. If the business does as well as expected, and there are no significant disagreements with investors, defects in the solicitation and sales process may go unnoticed. In such an instance, however, you will have been lucky rather than prudent.

A small amount of advance planning and caution can go a long way toward ensuring that fund raising will not become a hidden and potentially enormous liability. It is virtually certain that a disappointed investor will look to blame you — and to recover from you. Even a friend may become a formidable foe if the amount of money at stake is significant.

For additional resources on how to finance your business, refer to Appendix D.

Avoid Complexity

Because you are starting a business at home, seek simplicity. The law provides enormous opportunity for creativity and complexity. In most cases, however, your home-based business can avoid such complexity, as well as the expense and delay that often accompanies it.

As your business grows, your need for legal advice and assistance may also grow. Business relationships with customers and suppliers should be defined by written agreements. Short, form agreements or longer, custom agreements can be used, depending upon the situation. In each case, however, the key will be making the rights and responsibilities of the people involved clear.

With a modicum of prudent advice from a knowledgeable lawyer, you can make the law work to your benefit and avoid having to spend time and money correcting problems. This will enable you to spend more time and money on what really matters — your business.

Mile Post

The government has many interests in your business activities. By providing the government with the information and fees it requires by law and regulation, you will gain the protection and assistance of the government, rather than its suspicion and scrutiny.

Recordkeeping and Taxes

Recordkeeping

Recordkeeping is an important requirement for all businesses, and for many businesses, an accurately kept checkbook showing all expenses and income may be all that is necessary. However, it is wise to consult with an accountant early in the life of your new business so that he or she can help you determine how extensive a recordkeeping system is advisable for your business.

The ideal recordkeeping system is simple, accurate, and in compliance with federal and state tax requirements. The type of business — sole proprietorship, partnership, or corporation — and the particular needs and nature of the home business you have selected will determine what recordkeeping is necessary.

Well-organized and well-kept records will help you to monitor and evaluate the operations and progress of your new business and will enable you to prepare accurate tax returns. They also will not interfere with the most important aspect of your home-based business — running it.

Taxable Year

For tax purposes, business records are based on a one-year period, which is considered its taxable year. A taxable year may be a calendar year or a fiscal year consisting of any twelve consecutive months. In most cases, it will be a calendar year, beginning January 1st and ending December 31st. In some cases, the Internal Revenue Service (IRS) places restrictions on the use of noncalendar years for tax purposes.

A taxable year is established when a company files its first federal income tax return. Thereafter, it must continue to use this tax year, unless it obtains permission from the IRS to change it.

Accounting Methods

There are two basic accounting methods which are used to record business transactions — the cash method and the accrual method.

Cash Method

The cash method is based on reporting income when money is actually received and reporting expenses when bills are actually paid. Most small businesses are advised to use the cash method and post income and expenses on their books at the time money actually changes hands. The cash method is ideally suited to service-type businesses that have no product to buy, sell, or inventory. Those that have inventory may have some problems in isolating costs, sales, and profits on a cash basis.

> As an example, if a company or partnership were on a January 1–December 31 calendar year for reporting their taxes and bought $5,000 worth of product (inventory) in December and sold it in the January–March period the following year, they would have to book the cost of sales (purchase of products) in one year and the actual sales the following year. If they were using the accrual method they would just show the purchase of product in one year (inventory asset) and the sale and cost of those sales (product shipped) the following year. This would reflect a truer picture of their profit or loss in the year the sales took place.

Having said that the accrual method would show a truer picture for handling costs, such as product purchased in the period they are sold, it is still recommended that small home-based businesses use the cash method even if they are dealing with a product. The accounting becomes so much easier and in the final analysis does not affect the bottom line profit or loss.

The IRS does not allow the following taxpayers to use the cash method of accounting for tax purposes:

- Corporations (other than S corporations)
- Partnerships that have a corporation (other than an S corporation) as a partner
- Tax shelters

Accrual Method

In the accrual method, income is reported when it is earned, regardless of whether payment has actually been received and expenses are reported when they are actually incurred. The accrual method of accounting gives a truer picture of income and expenses for the reporting period.

Businesses may use either accounting method or a combination of the two, but they must apply the accounting method chosen consistently, so that the records clearly reflect income.

If, however, a company's income is derived from the production, purchase, or sale of merchandise and inventory is a material factor in determining income, it is required to keep inventory records to reflect income accurately and to use the accrual method to record purchases and sales.

As a practical matter, sales that have not been collected and inventory on hand may be recorded only once a year at the end of your accounting period.

Bookkeeping

There are two bookkeeping systems — the single-entry system and the double-entry system. The single-entry system is simpler, but the double-entry system, although more complex, assures better accuracy and control.

Single-entry System

Single-entry bookkeeping concentrates on the profit and loss statement and not on the balance sheet. It is a partial system that records the flow of income and expense, using a monthly summary of receipts and a monthly check disbursements journal.

Double-entry System

A double-entry system involves keeping journals and ledgers. Transactions are entered in a journal and then, at certain times, the totals are posted to ledger accounts showing income, expenses, assets, liabilities, and net worth. The system is self-balancing because each transaction is shown as a debit entry in one account and a credit entry in another. Since total debits must always equal total credits, a double-entry system will clearly show any errors that have been made.

At the end of an accounting period, a profit and loss statement is prepared that reflects current operations. A balance sheet is also prepared that shows the overall financial position of the business.

Checking Account

It is essential that you open and maintain a separate checking account for your new business. All receipts should be deposited in that checking account and all disbursements should be made from it. The cancelled checks are proof of a business' expenses. Avoid making checks payable to "cash" or to yourself, except for income withdrawals. Payments from petty cash should be documented by petty cash slips and receipts.

Cash Receipts Journal

A cash receipts journal lists receipts as they occur from each customer or client. The date, name and amount received are entered in this journal. A further breakdown of each receipt can be made separating the sale, freight, sales tax, material, etc.

Check Disbursements Journal

Regardless of whether you are using a single- or double-entry bookkeeping system, checks on your business account should be entered in a check disbursements journal.

The check disbursements journal allows you to keep track of total expenses, while breaking them down into categories. It is simply an analysis of your disbursement of checks. Each check is listed by date, check number, and payee. The amount of the check is entered in one column and then entered again under an appropriate column heading set up according to the type of cash expenditure. The journal may be handwritten or, in a business which has a large number of transactions, it may be created by a mechanical system (available at office supply stores), or by a computer.

At the end of the accounting period, the individual columns are totaled. The total expenditures can be determined for the period and also for the categories into which they fall. You can use this information to determine whether your expenses (for telephone, travel, office supplies, etc.) are within your original estimates. If they are running significantly higher, you may wish to review them and adjust your original estimates or reduce the expenditures.

At the end of a tax year, the cash receipts journal and the check disbursements journal are summarized to help in preparing a financial statement for the business and projections of operations for the following year. The summaries of the journals will also prove useful in preparing income tax returns.

In summary, the basic books of account are:

- Business checkbook
- Cash receipts journal
- Check disbursements journal
- General ledger (only for a double-entry system)

For more information regarding business records, contact your state's revenue or tax department, and see federal *Publication 334, Tax Guide for Small Business*. To determine which kind of recordkeeping system will best suit your business needs, you may wish to talk with your accountant.

Office supply stores sell a variety of complete bookkeeping systems as well as any recordkeeping forms and other materials you may need. If you work with a computer, you may want to consider using a simple bookkeeping software package.

Computer Programs

There are several computer programs that can be loaded into your computer that can make record keeping much easier for a small home-based business. This software allows you to enter your daily, weekly, and monthly transactions while providing you with accurate records, summaries, and quarterly and annual tax information.

Records for Employers

You are considered an employer if you pay someone to work for you or you are incorporated and pay yourself wages. You are then required to keep additional payroll records, which will reflect wages paid and tax withheld.

All records which support your tax returns, as well as the tax returns themselves, should be kept for at least three years — four years for employer information — after the return is filed.

As an employer, one of your important tax duties is to withhold federal and state taxes from your employees' wages. In addition, depending on the state you do business in, you may also have to pay unemployment insurance monies to your state.

You must also maintain records that show you have reviewed documents which identify each employee and that they are eligible to work in the United States.

Taxes

As an operator of a small business, you will have to report your income and pay taxes on the profits you may make.

If you are operating your home-based business as a sole proprietorship, the income and expenses of the business are reported on your personal income tax return.

If you are operating as a partnership, a separate partnership tax return should be filed and each partner's share of the profit or loss of the partnership should be reported on his or her individual tax return.

If you are operating as an S corporation, a separate S corporation tax return should be filed and each investor's share of the profit or loss of the corporation should be reported on each investor's individual income tax return.

If you are operating as a regular corporation, a separate corporation tax return should be filed. If your corporation makes a profit, taxes must be paid by the corporation on the profit. Important points to consider if you are setting up your business as a corporation are:

- Losses of a corporation remain within the tax structure and cannot be deducted by the shareholders.
- Profits of a corporation are taxed at the corporate level and again at the individual level, if they are paid to the shareholders as dividends.

Federal Identification Number

A federal employer identification number (FEIN) is required for partnerships and corporations. An FEIN is also required if you are a sole proprietor who pays wages to one or more employees. An FEIN can be obtained by filing federal *Form SS-4, Application for Employer Identification Number*, with the Internal Revenue Service.

Sales and Use Taxes

Businesses that sell goods or taxable services in a state which has a sales tax are responsible for charging, collecting, and paying the state's sales and use tax. You are usually liable for the payment of these taxes whether or not they have been collected. Information on these taxes, instructions, and an application for registering as a vendor can be obtained from your state's sales and use tax bureau or office.

General Employer Responsibilities

If you hire anyone to help operate your new business or if you are operating under a corporate structure and you yourself are on the payroll as an employee, you will have certain tax and insurance responsibilities.

Withholding Tax

You are responsible for withholding taxes from the wages of employees and for reporting and paying the taxes withheld in a timely manner. It is important to remember that if the tax laws require you to withhold income tax, you must pay taxes whether you have actually withheld them or not.

Unemployment Insurance

If you pay wages, you may be subject to federal and state unemployment insurance laws, and you must register with the Internal Revenue Service, as well as with your state's department of labor or employment security.

Workers' Compensation and Disability Benefits

As a new employer, be aware of your obligations regarding the disability benefits and workers' compensation insurance required for your employees. Information about these benefits and the forms needed to apply for them are available through private insurance carriers.

When starting your new home-based business, bear in mind that the recordkeeping system should be sufficient to properly determine the status of your business, while at the same time supplying the necessary information for any tax or regulatory agencies. Keep your records as simple as possible and keep your focus on running your business.

Mile Post

The purpose in starting your new business is to profit from it and enjoy it, not to be overwhelmed with recordkeeping. Simple, well-kept records can help make this a reality.

A Tour of 175 Home Business Ideas

The business ideas presented in this chapter can help you get started in a home-based, money-making venture of your own. While reading through each business description, keep in mind that products and services can be sold together and that several business ideas can be combined and changed to suit individual needs and interests.

When deciding on the business that seems right for you, also look to businesses operated outside the home for ideas. Often, businesses run from rented office or retail space can be adapted for home-based operation.

The business headings that follow have been arranged alphabetically by subject category. In some cases, business descriptions form their own subject category and therefore stand alone. Under most business subject categories, however, you will find descriptions of other product and service businesses, as well as occupations, that are related to the main subject category.

While reading through these business and occupation descriptions, if you develop some additional ideas, jot them down for your own future reference. In all cases, keep an open mind and you will most likely find a business or occupation that is right for you.

Automobiles

The automobile has become a necessity of life for most Americans and with this necessity comes the need for accessories, replacement parts, and other products and services. If you like to tinker with cars, why not turn one of your favorite pastimes into a home-based business? Consider some of the auto-related businesses and occupations discussed below.

Car Pools

People living in the suburbs usually need a car to commute to their place of employment. With gas prices getting higher each day, car pooling can become an economical option for these people. Most often, however, these commuters do not have the time or the facilities to organize their own rides. For a fee, you can locate and put together commuting partners. As people change their residence and jobs quite frequently these days, this is an area with potential turnover.

Car Sound System Installation

Whether it's rock and roll, classical music, or radio talk shows, part of the American driving experience is the car sound system. Become a distributor of automobile stereo radios, tape decks, and CD players, and install them in your driveway or garage. Place your name with stores that sell the equipment and with car dealerships that might require your services.

Chauffeur

If you have a car and are a good driver, start your own chauffeuring service. You don't have to own a limousine to be able to drive people in comfort to and from the airport or wherever else they wish to go. Check with your state's department of motor vehicles to ensure that you acquire the proper driver's license, then post your name and phone number around town. As your business grows, add more cars and drivers to your business and set yourself up as a dispatcher. Make sure you carry the proper insurance.

Classic Car Restoration

Collectors of classic and vintage cars do not always have the facilities or the know-how to restore the automobiles they enjoy collecting and driving. If you have a talent for rebuilding and tuning up old engines, put this to work for you. Spare parts and accessories for these older car models are also often very hard to find. With a little research and investigation, you can become a supplier of these hard-to-find parts. If you want to limit your investment, specialize in only one series of cars, one model, or one model for a particular year.

Car Driver

How about delivering new or just-purchased cars to their destinations? Often, car dealerships call around their regional area to find models in particular colors or with special options that are requested by customers. When located, these cars must be driven to the dealership that made the request. If you like to drive, check out car dealerships in your area that may need this service.

Driving Instructor

Think you are a good driver? Then register with a local driving school or motor vehicle bureau and take to the road as a driving instructor. There are students who need instruction from the basics up; foreign drivers who need a U.S. license; and those who have lost their licenses for one reason or another and need to start the process again.

With the current standard being automatic transmissions, you can specialize in manual transmission operation and attract those would-be car owners who want to learn to drive a "clutch." Start out part-time and slowly increase your hours before you commit yourself full-time.

Mobile Car Wash

From the back of your station wagon, van, or truck, you can operate your own car-washing service. Drive around residential neighborhoods and corporate parks and place flyers on car windshields to get car owners' attention. Also look for franchise opportunities in this area.

Used Car Evaluators

Used car evaluators provide a much needed service to purchasers of second-hand cars. With equipment, such as an engine compression tester and mechanical know-how, you can set yourself up to test used cars before buyers put their money down on cars that may not be worth the purchase price. Place your ad in the classified section of your local newspaper, near the used car section. Training is available from a used-car buying service if you want to associate and become part of such an established business.

Beauty and Health

As people strive for ways to improve their appearance, the health and beauty industry has become a booming business. Look for both products and services in this area as the basis of a profitable business. Specialize in care for men, women, or children, and take your business into peoples' homes for personal make-overs and beauty product parties. Advertise your business in local publications; or set yourself up as a manufacturer's representative and have clients referred to you by a parent company. The number of possible business ideas in this area is almost limitless. Here are just a few.

Beauty Products

Develop your own line of all natural beauty products. If you have a family beauty secret, try putting it on the market. Some people have found great success by manufacturing their great aunt's or other relative's formula for a moisturizing cream. Perhaps you, too, have a family product that other people might like to use. Determine if regulatory approval may be necessary before you start.

Beauty Products Representative

Selling beauty products from your home base — in your home or in the home of your customer or at small party gatherings. There are several cosmetic companies that market their line of products through representatives that set up their business at home. Some of these companies market through a multi-level marketing system.

Cosmetics Distributor

Almost everyone has heard of the Avon lady who travels door to door selling beauty products and accessories. You can become a cosmetics distributor for companies such as Avon and Mary Kay, whose representatives sell in local areas. If you prefer, you can arrange cosmetic parties where you offer facials and makeovers for customers interested in buying your products.

Hair Stylist — Mobile

Haircutting for men and women in the privacy of their homes or offices is a luxury service for busy, active people. The necessary tools and supplies are minimal. Sick or elderly people, who are housebound, can be particularly good customers. Check also with local hospitals and convalescent homes that may allow you to bring your services to their patients. Or, you can develop a following of busy executives who would enjoy such a service in their offices on a regular schedule.

Be sure to first check out any regulatory licensing requirements in your state. Also, there are franchising opportunities in this area if you're interested.

Health Products

Become a supplier of natural food products and vitamins. Sell door to door or set up racks in retail outlets. You can carry just one company's products or expand to distribute the products of several companies. Manufacturers usually advertise that they are seeking distributors in business or trade magazines.

Image Consultant

One secret to personal success is the image you present. Many business executives, public figures, and entertainers feel that their image enhances their chances for success. If you have a knowledge of makeup, hair design, clothing style and fit, as well as body language, you can become an image consultant and help your clients acquire the appearance and poise they desire. Contacts at beauty salons, clothing, and shoe stores will help you to gain the confidence of your clients.

Manicurist

Manicures and pedicures for beautiful hands and feet are always in demand. Perform your service at your home or in your clients' homes, and be sure to check whether a license is required. You can distribute nail products and lotions as part of your service as well. Training is readily available through courses or on-the-job training.

Masseur/Masseuse

Massage and New Age body work can be performed in your home, if you have a quiet space, or bring your service to your clients' homes. Select taped music to enhance the relaxed and healthful atmosphere your service provides. Training and licensing is usually required, so contact the proper state agency for information.

Bed and Breakfast

Bed and breakfast inns are being successfully operated out of family homes all over the United States. All you need is a spare bedroom or two and the desire to meet new people. Registration with a bed and breakfast organization will help you get started. Find out about historical sites in your area and gather pamphlets and brochures for your guests along with the numbers of local transportation services and restaurants. If you live near large corporate offices, investigate listing your bed and breakfast with them. More and more major corporations are exploring the bed and breakfast alternative for their traveling employees or guests. Set up a morning menu and provide a bright and cheerful place for breakfast. If you have a lovely garden, you can feature "breakfast on the terrace" as one of your seasonal attractions.

To find out more about the bed and breakfast business, you may want to obtain a copy of *Open Your Own Bed and Breakfast* by Barbara Notarius. This book provides answers to the many questions you may have when considering opening your home as a bed and breakfast. The book is available in bookstores or by calling (800) 982-BOOK.

Bicycle Repairs

Set up a bicycle repair shop in your garage or basement. Place your name with local retailers that sell bicycles and with organizations that sponsor bicycling tours. With oil prices soaring, the bicycle may find its way back as a major source of transportation.

Boating and Yachting

Depending on your location, businesses that provide products and services to boat owners can enjoy seasonal or year-round markets. If you live near the water, there is a profit to be made from both sailing and motor vessels. Advertise your business at local marinas and yacht clubs.

Bottom Cleaning

Cleaning of both motor and sail boats helps to cut down on the drag caused by marine growth that clings to the bottoms of boats anchored or moored in salt-water harbors. If you are a licensed scuba diver, you can arrange to clean several boats at a time in one area. Yacht clubs that often have racing-class sail boats are ideal places to advertise your service. You can schedule monthly maintenance and develop a year around income. Once you have proven the quality and dependability of your work, you may find that word of mouth referrals will keep you busy.

Charter Captain

Yacht owners who charter their boats to vacationers need captains who can navigate the waters in which their boats will be sailed. These can be tropical harbors, ocean coasts, lakes, or rivers. If you live in an area where people spend their leisure time on the water, this may be an ideal service business for you. Offer your services during the day only, or make yourself available for overnight cruises. Check with the U.S. Coast Guard for permit and licensing requirements.

Crew Member

If you're not quite ready to captain a boat, you might consider offering your services as a crew member. Boat owners who need to transport their vessels from one point to another for storage or sale, but who cannot do it themselves because of time restrictions, seek reliable crew members to do the job. If you know of captains who do such work, place your name with them. Advertise in marine publications, and look for ads and notices placed by boat owners who are looking for such services.

Garbage Pick-up

Garbage pick-up is a service that can be provided to boat owners who live on their boats during weekends and vacations. A small motorboat can be used to pick up household garbage, which is then carted away, on land, to a local garbage dump.

Harbor Food Service

Enterprising individuals in some ports have started food delivery services in harbor marinas. These include gourmet foods and appetizers, as well as hot coffee and fresh baked goods delivered with the Sunday morning newspaper. Similar to a mobile restaurant, you could pack your goods into a small motorboat and go from boat to boat announcing your menus. After a long sail to visit a distant port, your clients will be rewarded with a delicious meal delivered to their boat. These services are welcome and business picks up fast.

Instrument Installation

Boat owners are continually upgrading their equipment. Take advantage of the opportunities available in this area and install marine instruments and accessories at marinas and boat yards. Place your name with equipment distributors and marina owners. You can work for individual boat owners or take jobs on a freelance basis from boat yard management companies.

Name Painting

One of the favorite pastimes of boat owners is the naming of their boats. If you have a flair for print and signing, put this talent to use painting names on boats. Many styles and sizes of print can be used. As your business grows, take photos of the boats you have worked on and place these in a portfolio to show prospective clients. Place your name with yacht brokers, boat yards, and boat supply stores.

Sail Maker

Sail making and repair sound like an art from days gone by, but the services of these artists are still needed today. Any yacht club or marina that harbors sailing vessels will have torn sails that need repair. Since sails are made from many square feet of material, be certain you have enough space for work and storage.

Sailing Instructor

From young children to older retired couples, people want to learn how to sail . If qualified, give lessons in wind surfing, racing techniques, and navigational cruising.

Water Taxi

Water taxis provide a much needed service to boat owners who require transportation from their boats to the towns they are visiting. Check with the U.S. Coast Guard for required licenses, get a marine radio and call sign, and take your water-bound passengers to their destinations. Advertise your service in cruising guides, marinas, and yacht clubs.

Business Services

Today, more than ever before, both large and small businesses are using services offered on the outside to help with the day-to-day running of office affairs. If you have a skill that can be offered to the business sector, but don't want full- or part-time employment, consider offering your services independently from your own home office.

Look through the Yellow Pages to find a list of companies in your area and send out a mailing. Business supply stores and other companies offering products to businesses are good contacts. Place your name with these companies and ask for referrals if companies request the services you offer. Print cards and professional brochures and canvas your local area, leaving your card and brochure at reception desks. While you're there, get the name of the office manager or other company officer, and keep a record of these names for future follow-up phone calls. The business and occupation descriptions listed below are opportunities that exist in today's business world. You can use one of these ideas or apply a particular skill of your own towards opening your own home-based business service.

Benefits Consultant

With so many rules and regulations governing the business activities of small businesses, the owners of such businesses sometimes find the required forms and filings overwhelming to complete. Knowledgeable human resources executives are particularly suited to provide these services to small business owners. The owners usually save money, in-house staff and can devote more time to running their businesses.

Bookkeeper

Bookkeeping is another business service you can offer from your home. Contact the federal government and your state's department of taxation and finance for informational brochures to help you understand the different methods of record-keeping and taxation. Look into courses on small business operation and record-keeping to gain further information and expertise. With the rise in the number of entrepreneurial businesses, your services will surely be welcomed.

Bulk Mailing Services

A service for small companies that have periodic or regular small quantity bulk mailings. The service company would advice the company on regulations that govern their mailings. Different sorting techniques can be applied to save the mailer monies and bring the mailings costs down. Pick up and delivery to the U.S. Postal Service could also be part of the bulk mailing services.

Mailing List Maintenance

Mailing lists are the basis of direct-mail promotions for many companies. If you have a computer with ample document storage, you can maintain mailing lists for advertising and promotional purposes. This entails adding new names and addresses, updating existing addresses, and deleting duplicate names. As part of your service, you can offer printed labels and subject searches.

Manufacturers Representative

There are many manufacturers of products that are looking for a representative to sell products in a particular area. Usually the fees paid are commissions on the sales you make. Representing for several companies that are not competing is entirely possible. Most representatives work from home.

Marketing Consultant

If you have had great experience in the corporate world in marketing and sales, you might want to apply those talents on a consulting basis to companies seeking such services. You can develop several small companies as clients who use your services several hours per week. Another method is to sell your consulting services on a project basis. Be cautious in using this approach as you may have to devote all your time to one company to the detriment of your client base.

Medical Transcription Service

These services can be provided for doctors either working from your home or at the doctors office. A multiplicity of insurance forms, medical summary letters and reports are all part of a medical transcription service business. There are training courses available for the home business entrepreneur that needs help in setting up this kind of business.

Messenger/Courier Service

Hand deliver messages and packages to businesses in your town. If you have a car, you can deliver to businesses in neighboring towns and cities as well. As your business grows, hire couriers to help you with either the local or out-of-town jobs.

Resumé Preparer

Resumé preparation is a much tougher job than most people realize. That's why there are so many books on the subject. However, you don't have to be an expert in career counseling to help someone put their employment history together in a concise and legible form, though it does help if you have some background in this area. You will also need an excellent typewriter or word processor with a letter-quality printer. Post flyers and advertise your service in employment agencies and on the bulletin boards of local colleges and trade schools.

Telephone Answering Service

For business owners who are not always available to answer their clients' calls, telephone answering services are often preferred to telephone answering machines. Doctors, for example, who cannot be at their offices at all times, need the personal touch of a telephone operator to screen calls for emergencies. Other people simply prefer that their clients speak with a person, not a machine. Invest in a telephone board that can handle many phone lines at one time. Organize yourself so you have a quick and accurate method of recording messages, and you're on your way!

Word Processing

Word processing is another possible business opportunity, if you own a computer. Similar to typing services, word processing services offer clean and well-typed material on paper copy or on computer diskettes. You can offer this service to both the educational and business sectors.

Children's Services and Products

As long as there have been children, there has been a need for child-related services and products. With so many mothers working long hours, both inside and outside the home, the need for day care, babysitting, or other child-related activities have been on the rise. If you enjoy being with children, perhaps a child service is right for you. There are many books available to give you suggestions on activities children enjoy. These cover programs for all ages. Also, the Red Cross offers first aid and accident prevention courses that can be a valuable resource to anyone interested in babysitting and child care. Parents are always interested in learning about new products which can help further their children's educational development and recreational enjoyment. If you are creative and have your own children's book, toy, or accessory idea, then you very well may be interested in this type of home-based business.

Babysitting

Babysitting services usually require that you, as the sitter, go into a child's home. A more profitable and professional approach to traditional babysitting, however, is to become a babysitting broker, with a registry of babysitters on call whom you have checked out thoroughly. The registry can consist of sitters who range in age from teenagers to grandmothers. All must be preapproved and qualified for their assignments. Because your clients are dealing with a registry, they are assured of getting a competent sitter when they need one. Maintain a record of each sitter's background, qualifications, and experience so that it can be conveyed if requested by a client. After a sitting assignment, check with the client for feedback on the sitter and customer satisfaction. As a broker, you should receive 10% to 15% of what the sitter earns.

Children's Entertainer

Are you skilled as a magician or a clown, or do you keep children spellbound as you tell stories? Schools, boy and girl scout troops, churches, libraries, and other organizations sponsoring children's activities are always looking for people to entertain at special events. Place your name with several of these organizations and post flyers at party shops. Don't forget to stay in touch with the children's party planners — these party organizers like to keep in touch with entertainers for parties they are arranging.

Children's Party Planner

If you enjoy children and are creative and imaginative, you have what it takes to become a children's party planner. Plan and organize birthdays and other children's parties to be held in your clients' homes, amusement parks, clubs, hotels, restaurants, or game rooms. Offer a wide variety of programs, products, and services geared to various age groups and interests. Party packages can be planned around specific themes, such as Disney characters, Sesame Street, sports, or Halloween; or feature an activity, such as artwork, simple handicrafts, or games. The important thing is that the client knows you can take charge of all aspects of the party and handle and provide whatever specific services that complement what they want to do themselves. Your services can include providing the food, decorations, table items, prizes and favors, imaginative games and activities, recorded or live children's music, personalized balloons, and other novel items that children enjoy. Develop a list of special children's entertainers, such as clowns, storytellers, magicians and musicians, and amusements such as kiddy or pony rides. You can have several party themes and a range of services, but try to develop these into standard party packages with different set costs.

Day Care Center

Small day care centers can be set up in the home with minimal investment. First check with local authorities that regulate child care services in your area to determine what licensing and other requirements you must comply with, and be sure that you meet these requirements. Consider whether you prefer caring for infants, toddlers, or pre-school children, or whether you want to specialize in before- or after school care for school-aged children. Consider the area of your home that you can devote to this business and what equipment and toys will be appropriate

If you think child care is the way you want to go, advertise your services in local publications. Register with local hotels and motels; put notices in pediatricians' offices, nursery and day care centers; and if there are any large corporations in your area, try giving the personnel department a ring. They may have some working mothers who need help. Post your name on the bulletin boards in office coffee or lunch rooms and mail out flyers.

Children's Products — Accessories and Toys

Children's accessories, such as crib and carriage quilts and blankets, pillows and matching wall hangings, are good ideas for a line of children's products. Personalized items, as well as those intended specifically for boys or girls can be featured. Clothing (sleepers, booties, sweaters) can also be made to match those items used in the nursery. There are many ideas that can be put to practical application here. Personalized diaper bags and carry-alls for mothers are excellent baby shower gift items and can be advertised as such. Offer gift certificates for your items and let the certificate holder order personalized items or select from a line of ready-made children's accessories.

Handcrafted toys are in great demand today as gift-givers search for unique items to present as gifts to their sons, daughters, nieces, nephews, etc. Items for young babies — rattles, soft cuddly stuffed animals, and developmental toys — sell in baby shops and at craft fairs. They are also popular items for mail-order catalogs.

Computers

Your personal home computer can be used in a number of ways to provide you with extra income to start a home-based business. New hardware and software products are continually reaching the market, ever increasing the range of possible income opportunities available to you. The day is closer than you may think when office workers will no longer commute to central locations, but will work at home and electronically telecommunicate with their main offices. Before you purchase any computer equipment or software, compare prices and shop around. Most importantly, be certain that you purchase materials which are compatible with each other. Research the potential for computer-based services in your area and after deciding on a particular service you can offer to potential clients, advertise in local publications and by sending out promotional letters. Here are some computer-oriented home business suggestions.

Animator

Produce software animation for advertisers putting materials on the Internet. Also use computer animation for the production of TV commercials or short documentaries.

CD-ROM Master Production

Produce CD-ROMs for music companies or other uses. Equipment cost can be expensive in setting up this business.

Computer Consultant

Computer consultants are in great demand as individuals and businesses recognize the time- and money-saving advantages offered by personal computers. If computers are your specialty, put your knowledge to work helping individuals and businesses decide on the equipment they should purchase as well as the software they should buy to suit the jobs they need to get done. Charge your clients on an hourly or project basis, depending on the amount of time and work necessary to complete each project. Obtain wholesale prices at computer stores and charge a commission on the hardware and software that you acquire for clients.

Computer Presentations

Companies who want to have their salesman or headquarter people make presentations on laptops or PCs will entertain giving that project to an outside specialist firm. Proficiency in making these presentations is necessary. Fees paid for this service are unusually high.

Computer Programmer

Computer programmers can generate programs for specific projects on their personal computers. Meet with prospective clients to evaluate their programming needs and the computer equipment they have available. Then, you can complete your work at home by preparing tailormade programs to suit any job and computer system. Small businesses as well as educational and institutional organizations may be your best clients. Place your name with suppliers of computer equipment and send out a mailing to organizations you have researched.

Computer Services

Maintain business records for small companies which cannot afford the time or overhead to do their own. Meetings to discuss services such as generation of pay-roll checks can be held at your clients' offices or in your home. If you have a spreadsheet program, sales projections can also be included as a service.

Computer Technical Writer

If you are good at technical writing, you might consider setting yourself up to provide those services to pharmaceutical or engineering companies. They can usually give you a steady stream of documents that have to be developed by these companies. The fees for such services would depend on how technical the information is that you have to incorporate in a brochure or document.

Computerized Accounting Service

Set up to do the accounting work for small businesses on your computer. Client company feeds you the documentation, your company produces the necessary P&Ls, balance sheets, and tax information.

Desktop Publishing

Desktop publishing businesses offer typesetting as well as graphic art services. Whether you choose to edit electronic manuscripts or design pamphlets and pro-motional brochures, the work can be done right in your home with page-making and graphics software and equipment. Invest in a quality laser printer to make your products competitive with typeset materials. Since computer-generated copy is less expensive to produce than copy produced by traditional typesetting methods, you have a built-in edge over your competition. To attract potential customers, design a brochure that shows off your design capabilities. Maintain a portfolio of your work to present at interviews with prospective clients.

Image Scanning Services

Although the price of scanning machines have gone down there still is a scanning service that small businesses can use. The convenience of such a service often overcomes pricing differentials for the person setting up such a business.

Internet Web Site Developer

Many desk top publishers are extending their talents to web site development for small and large companies. If you are very knowledgeable in the interaction between a web site and engines necessary to reach that site, this may be an excellent business for you. The design of the site and bringing out the reason for having the site should be important aspects of your marketing plan.

Personal Computer Instruction

For anyone who has tried to learn to operate his or her personal computer by reading the owner's manual, being able to ask a real-life person questions and advice is a godsend. If you have mastered the use of operating various PCs and software programs, you will find that your services are in great demand — from children's educational programs to financial spreadsheets. Advertise your service anywhere computers are sold as well as on local school and office bulletin boards.

Software Tester

Companies that produce software like to have that software tested in real applications. A person proficient in the use of different software packages can establish a business in testing software for the creators of that software.

Technical Support Provider

Set up business to provide computer technical support to businesses using computers or computer networks as part of their businesses. Some assistance via telephone can be accomplished, nevertheless proximity to the client is usually essential.

Used Computer Dealer

Selling used computers to the person or business that does not require the latest computers or software is a simple home-based business. Some inventory may be necessary. You may be able to sell from a simple catalog and have the refurbisher hold the inventory.

Used Computers

Purchase of used computers from leasing companies, refurbishing them and selling them to other companies who specialize in used computers. Can also be done with individuals who want to sell their computers.

Consulting and Professional Services

As a result of downsizing or cyclical seasonal or economic changes some professionals have found themselves separated from their employment. This separation can be a shock to the engineer, lawyer, accountant, marketing or advertising executive, who expected to stay in a particular field where he or she was educated, trained, and employed. Many look for new jobs in the same field while others spread into similar or allied fields seeking employment. A growing number of professionals have decided they have had enough of employment that is too unstable and have set up shop as home-based entrepreneurs. Possibly you, too may want to direct your talents either part-time or full-time into a home business. Some of the business ideas in this section may jog your mind into thinking of a business that appeals to you. Keep in mind that you can use your background and combine it with fresh ideas to develop an altogether new service or a service with a new slant on it or, you may want to take this opportunity to make a complete career change, and turn a favorite hobby in to a home business such as catering, or landscaping.

Accountant

Because there are many new businesses springing up, there is quite a market for accounting services. New business owners need help setting up and maintaining their books and preparing tax returns. If you are an accountant, you can maintain an office in your home and visit your clients' homes and offices to supply accounting services. Personal income tax preparation is another highly necessary and much-in-demand service. To best organize both your clients' files and your own, invest in a personal computer and some accounting and recordkeeping software.

Architect

There are many areas of design that can become lucrative specialties for the home-based architect. You already have the training and probably most of the equipment and tools you will need. Consider directing your efforts into designing single family homes, retail stores, kitchens, additions, renovations, small commercial buildings, or indoor pools as a specialty. Designs can be sold for a fee with additional income for supervising construction or obtaining contractors.

Career Counselor

Career counseling can be a rewarding experience. If you are retired, you can draw on your years of work experience and give younger and less-experienced job hunters advice. If you were employed by an employment agency or corporate personnel department, you may find career counseling from your home a satisfying and lucrative experience.

Copywriter

Advertising copy, letters, reports — you'd be surprised how many business owners need the help of good copywriters. If you are talented and experienced in writing, put this to work for you. Your clients can include business owners, advertising agencies, and publishing companies. Just demonstrate your writing expertise by composing a compelling promotional letter explaining what you can do, and how your skills benefit your clients, and you'll be on your way.

Engineer

Whatever your engineering background is you can use the analytical training you received plus your engineering specialty in a number of ways. Selling your services back to your former employer on an hourly or project-by- project basis can be a cost saver for them and an income producer for you. Also, you can sell these same services to additional companies that are in a similar field to your former employer. If you are a civil engineer you might try contracting your services to your local municipality or county on a part-time basis. Many engineering projects can be solved from the comfort of your home for clients in industry and government. Keep in mind that many of our country's most successful companies began in engineers' homes.

Financial Planner

Small business owners usually need help in planning the financial needs of their company and personal activities. A financial planner brings this information to the business owner. Also, with knowledge of the multiple sources that an individual can invest monies in, for retirement or a college education for children, the financial planner can have both individual and business clients. A thorough knowledge of investing in many different instruments is necessary for the planner.

Import/Export Broker

A service for companies not familiar with the regulations that govern export or import regulations and procedures. Could be limited to just an advisory service or it could include handling and filing the proper paperwork.

Management Consultant

Many small and medium-sized businesses are looking for help in improving their business. They usually do not know where to turn for assistance. If you have an extensive background in business, are a good listener and problem-solver, you might enjoy providing overall business advice to clients. If you have a background in a specialized area, concentrate on that as a consultant.

Ask your friends and former associates for suggestions of who might be interested in your services. Then follow through by contacting those prospects, mentioning who referred you to them, and briefly explaining your background.

Prepare a short brochure or letter explaining your services and background and use this to reach these and other potential clients. You may also want to test mailing to a purchased list.

Marketing Consultant

If you have been marketing a product or service in the confines of a large corporation or advertising agency and now want to do it on your own or possibly as a part-time endeavor, why not become a marketing consultant? Many small and medium-sized businesses seek such assistance to help them plan and implement marketing programs. To meet potential clients, attend or speak at local association meetings of industries you would like to serve. Talk to people there about how you can help companies sell more of their products or services. Then when you have arranged presentation meetings with interested prospects, be prepared to discuss the specific results you achieved for other companies.

Personnel Manager

The amount of paperwork and personnel forms that have to be completed by businesses has become enormous. If you are familiar with these responsibilities and the laws and regulations governing how they must be done, you might want to set up a service managing this paperwork for others. If you have had a lot of practice interviewing and hiring employees, consider creating a personnel search firm or personnel agency. Check if licensing is necessary.

Publicist

The interaction between the client and the publicist can take place anywhere. The interaction between the publicist and representatives of newspapers, magazines, radio or television is usually via phone or by the written word. Hence, it is natural to operate this type of business from home. Many do. Take Marisa who had her first child and had to transfer her publicist work from the office to home. Her work continued for clients via her home computer, the telephone and her facsimile and telephone answering machines. Even after her second child, she continued to keep her media contacts active and productive.

Dance

Many people of all ages enjoy dance. If you are particularly good on your feet, select your music and start teaching. Turn your basement or extra room into a studio or, if you have no space at home, try renting space in local churches, schools, and office buildings. Classes can be private or offered as group instruction. Sponsor recitals or social dances at the end of your sessions. These are fun for your students and good promotional events for you. If you're good at putting dance steps together, offer your services as a choreographer to local dance and theater groups. Post flyers in local dance equipment shops. Advertise in local publications, and check with schools that may be looking for the services of private dance instructors.

Ballet, Jazz, and Tap Instruction

If you have danced professionally or in the theater, perhaps you'd be interested in teaching your craft to children or adults in your home. Many parents believe ballet is an essential for the development of grace and poise. Other students may want to work towards their future in a dance career. Either way, there is a market and a demand for good classical dance teachers.

Social and Ballroom Dancing

Couples not dancing are usually dying to get out on the floor, but their problem is they don't know how to do the traditional or contemporary social dances. These people would jump at the chance to learn how to dance in your private home studio. If taking people into your home is not convenient, go to your clients' homes or organize dancing parties in a rented space. Collect music for your particular specialty. If contemporary dancing is your choice, be sure to keep up with the newest songs and steps.

Education

If you have a teaching degree, or knowledge in a specialized area, you can make the opportunities discussed below work for you. Many people have taken students into their homes to give them extra help with schoolwork or to offer instruction in something completely new. (These services can also be brought to your clients' homes or offices.) Educational services can be advertised through local school systems or inexpensive local publications. If you are certified in a particular area, advertise this prominently. You can also register with teaching organizations that will refer you to clients; or you can set up a registry and refer clients to your prescreened staff of tutors.

ESL Instruction

English as a second language (ESL) is a popular phrase in minority communities in the United States today. Many adults and children coming to live in this country need help with speaking, reading, and writing English. It is helpful to speak your students' native language, so if you are fluent in a language other than English, especially Spanish or Japanese, put that knowledge to work for you.

Music Instruction

Musical instrument instruction and voice lessons can be given in your home or those of your clients. Students, both young and old, are interested in voice coaching or in private lessons in piano, guitar, flute, harmonica, percussion instruments — you name it. Arrange for recitals to give your students opportunities to show off their talents. Put your name in with local schools and post your services at local music and instrument rental outlets.

Tutor

Tutoring in subjects from the grade school level on up is always in demand. Math, reading comprehension, science, and foreign-language instruction are some of the more popular areas. You can also offer specialized instruction to help students prepare for their college boards. Some tutors visit their clients' homes; others prefer to have their students come to them. The arrangement depends on what you and your clients agree upon.

Event Planning

Be an event planner for weddings, birthdays, graduations, retirement parties, anniversaries, and other special occasions. You will need floral, catering, party supply, and restaurant/hall contacts so you can offer quick and efficient service. Make creative themes one of your specialties and find outlets for the supplies you will need. Establish a rate schedule that includes per-guest prices for several party themes. Or organize one-of-a-kind events for each client.

Exercise and Fitness

From aerobics to yoga, exercise instruction is more popular than ever. You can hold classes in your home or visit your students as a personal trainer. For exercise that requires extensive physical exertion, look into certification. Screen your clients carefully and request a doctor's written permission in some cases. It is also advisable to have your students sign releases before classes begin — these will protect you in the case of an accident. Since exercise classes usually take place over a series of weeks, plan your schedule and be sure to advertise in advance to allow enough time to fill your classes. Post flyers in sports equipment shops, doctors' offices, public libraries, and other local gathering places.

Aerobic Classes

With an assortment of slow and fast-paced music, you can put together a few routines for aerobic exercise. If you don't have enough space in your home, look into renting space in local buildings, such as churches and schools. Invest in a good sound system to be sure your music is loud and clear, and then start exercising.

Bicycling Tours

If you like to bicycle, why not organize and run bicycling tours? Tours can be conducted locally or taken to resort areas as longer trips. Plan out several routes. Check restaurant and sleeping accommodations and set up reservations in advance. If your clients do not have their own bicycles, make an agreement with a local bicycle shop so you can get bicycles when you need them.

Exercise for Pregnant Women

If you are a registered nurse or obstetrics nurse, consider giving exercise classes for expecting mothers. Group classes in your home can be fun, and routines can focus on prenatal exercise as well as getting back in shape after the baby is born. Be sure to get the names and phone numbers of your students' doctors.

Exercise for Senior Citizens

Specialized exercises for the elderly are becoming more and more popular as people live longer, more active lives. Exercises can include slow-paced aerobic dance, yoga, walking, and calisthenics that offer not only physical activity, but social stimulation as well. Post your name with local senior citizen centers.

Tennis Instructor

If you are into the tennis tournament circuit, here's one area in which you can make some extra money, especially if you have acquired professional status. Rent time at local tennis courts and give private and group lessons. Teach beginners as well as advanced students, and offer tournaments to give your students a chance to show off their skills. Advertise by posting flyers in sports equipment shops and supermarkets. Place inexpensive ads in local publications.

Walking

Weather-permitting, of course, walking can be a great source of exercise. Take people on walking tours of your hometown, local parks and recreation areas, and places of historical interest. Show your clients the best ways to get maximum exercise benefits from their walking, and put it together with fun. If you walk several times a week, perhaps each week can feature a different theme or route.

Yoga

Yoga and other Oriental exercise programs are great sources of relaxation as well as discipline and exercise. All you need is a working knowledge of the exercises and a quiet space. Classes can be held during the day for harried mothers whose children are at school, or in the evening for stressed commuters.

Fashion

If you make clothes at home for yourself and your family, have you considered creating your own line of fashion designs? Boutiques and small clothing stores are always looking for new designs to attract customers. Specialize in clothing for children, teenagers, men or women, or design one garment that can be worn by anyone — just vary your size and color selections. Attract customers by displaying your clothes at craft fairs and street bazaars, and by mailing brochures.

Food

If you like to cook, and have a talent for preparing a particular food — foreign cuisine, pastries, baked goods, gourmet appetizers — you have one of the essential ingredients for starting your own food business. Food businesses can include both product- and service-oriented companies. If you are skilled at food presentation, you might be interested in a catering venture. If you are famous for your spicy Spanish appetizers, try selling these to specialty shops. Whatever you choose, your production should be kept fresh. Check out local zoning and health department regulations before you begin. You may have to invest in some regulation equipment to get a permit before you can begin operation.

Catering

If you can prepare tasty food and present it in an attractive manner, a home-based catering business is a great way to put your cooking talents to work for you. It is not necessary to be a gourmet chef. The important thing is to offer food that you can prepare well from quality ingredients at reasonable prices. Many people who lack the time or cooking expertise use small caterers to handle their at-home entertaining. Consider whether you want to offer complete meals, or choose a specialty such as appetizers, buffet meals, party foods, holiday specialties, ethnic dishes, or desserts. You can offer a set menu selection, or work with your clients to prepare themes and food selection. Whether you choose to handle large or small events, or both, depends on your experience and what you think you can handle. Small catering businesses usually grow by word-of-mouth. To get started, spread the word among your friends, but also try advertising in local publications.

Cooking Classes

Another way to put your cooking talents to work is to offer cooking classes in your home. This can be done with virtually no investment. One enterprising woman started a very successful cooking class business by teaching the newly arrived wives of Japanese businessmen to cook simple American meals. She lists her classes with Japanese corporations in her area and, since most of their personnel are here for only one or two years, there are always new students for her classes. Another way to specialize is to offer a series of classes for specific types of foods, such as Chinese food, Italian food, cakes and pies, holiday specialties, or gourmet meals; or you can offer classes for people with special dietary interests, such as vegetarians, weight watchers, diabetics, or people with food allergies. In most instances, the cost of the food being prepared is passed on to the students as part of the class fee. What you will need is ample working space and cooking utensils to outfit a class. The type of cooking you want to teach will determine how and where you should advertise. You can place ads in local publications, or you may publicize your classes at no cost by posting notices with special-interest groups, doctor's offices, weight clinics, or community bulletin boards.

Lunch Service

Prepare boxed lunches for office employees, school outings, company picnics, and sporting events in your home. Design a menu — with accompanying prices — that provides a selection to suit varying tastes. Research organizations that might use your service and send them a menu along with your promotional material.

Mobile Restaurant

The traveling restaurant, operated from the back of a truck or van, can pick up business in office parks, recreational areas, or ballparks. Permits are required for mobile restaurant operation, so check local regulations before starting such a business. Also look for franchise opportunities in this area.

Homemade Food Specialties

There are many success stories about people who started making cheesecakes, pies, cookies, or other food items in their homes and went on to become nationally known and highly successful. You can also turn your cooking talents into profit. Those outlets where food specialties are most often sought are restaurants, specialty stores, delicatessens, farm stands, and coffee houses. Make samples and bring them around. You can also advertise in local publications. The items listed below are just a few examples of the kinds of products that can be sold. Use your imagination. There's always room for something new, exciting, and delicious!

Baked Goods

Baked goods hot and fresh from the oven are tasty treats almost no one can resist. Pies, cakes, cookies, brownies, breads, and muffins are popular favorites. Your potential market would be coffee shops, delicatessens, and grocery stores that sell hot coffee in the morning. As your baked goods become part of the local morning coffee break, you will enjoy delicious profits.

Candy

Chocolates and candies can be sold as party favors or to local specialty shops. Create your own line of candies by using different patterns — animals, flowers, leaves, hearts, footballs, and dolls — to add diversity. Package your candies in brightly colored foils and papers that will attract attention and consider changing the foils and papers for special sales during different holidays.

Herbs

Herbs, spices, and condiments are sought after by restaurants looking for something different to attract customers. They are also the important ingredients that line the shelves of gourmet shops. If you have a special salad dressing recipe that everyone raves about, bottle it, and ask a few restaurant owners to give it a try.

Pastas

Fresh pasta and homemade sauces can be sold to local restaurants and gourmet shops. Try out your favorite recipe. It may become a hit.

Preserves

Jams, jellies, and other preserves are food items you can make in your own kitchen. If available, use fruit grown in your backyard as your primary ingredients. Look for new and tasty combinations to make your products special. Design fancy labels and use jars that give your preserves a fresh, homemade look.

Spiced Vinegars

Spiced vinegars can be made and bottled at home with homegrown herbs and spices. Look for interesting bottles and have a label designed and printed. If you have a special recipe, include it on the label. Or, create a small pamphlet that describes how your vinegar was made and give several recipes for its use.

Franchises

Franchise opportunities are available in almost every service or product area you can think of — the number of franchises is almost endless. When analyzing a franchise, bear in mind the advantages and disadvantages that usually go with the franchise. If you want some of the start up already done, some name recognition, and marketing procedures already in place, a franchise may be right for you. On the other hand, if you have limited funds and don't want to put up the usually required franchise fee, or don't want to be constrained by the franchise agreement's do's and don'ts, you may want to stay away from a franchise arrangement. To give you a representative sampling of the types of franchises available, see the list below. Keep in mind that some of these businesses — all of which can be operated from home — can be started without a franchise.

Accounting Management

This type of franchise covers a wide range of accounting applications from simple accounting and bookkeeping to taxes to full computer services. You should have a background in accounting, and a personal computer would be helpful for record-keeping and spreadsheet purposes.

Bath and Kitchen Repair

If you are a handyperson who wants to work from home, a franchise which offers the franchisee the ability to refinish and repair bath and kitchen fixtures might be just the thing.

Business Brokerage

List and sell going businesses. Clients come to your office or you visit their businesses. Training and support as well as some regional advertising are available.

Career Counseling

Franchises offer a program to market and administer career counseling, including manuals, client materials, and computer software. Intended for those who want to assist others in their career objectives. This type of counseling can range from relatively simple to very sophisticated. Educational background is important.

Carpet Cleaning

Carpet cleaning franchises specialize in carpets and other home cleaning services such as drapes and furniture. Some parent companies will sell equipment, others will direct you to the proper equipment. Often, these franchises offer assistance in management and advertising.

Commercial Cleaning

There are several franchises available that specialize in the cleaning of commercial space. These franchises help set you up and assist in training, management, and advertising. You could put together a small group of people who offer store cleaning on a regular basis. You'll find that many retailers and offices appreciate these services.

Diet Products

Diet product franchises include some or all of the following: weight control, behavior modification, nutrition counseling, and sale of vitamins, food supplements and foods. Usually, you will have to have some training from the parent company, and a background in nutrition or fitness training might be helpful.

Direct Mail

A direct-mail franchise is a low-overhead business in which people with diverse backgrounds have succeeded. Sales and management experience is helpful. Some companies offer on-going assistance after the franchise has been established.

Haircutting/Styling

A haircutting franchise can provide low-cost no-frills hair services for the entire family. Prices vary according to each type of hair service offered. Some franchises can be operated from a room set up at home for this purpose — others require a store outlet. Training and advertising assistance is included. Start-up assistance and an equipment purchase package is included in some programs. A word of caution: check regulatory agencies to find out about licensing and approvals.

Home Inspections

Home-inspection franchises which cater primarily to home buyers are available. Such clients are usually seeking an inspection and report on a single family home that they are contemplating buying. This type of franchise can be operated on a full- or part-time basis.

Lawn and Garden Care

There are many franchises that provide lawn services such as aeration, fertilization, and crabgrass, and weed and insect control. Most provide training and support to the franchisee. Some have detailed procedures and a format for doing business. These businesses are not just concerned with cutting lawns — they are directed toward maintaining good healthy lawns.

Maid Service

A maid service franchise usually includes an extensive training and support program, and provides services to both domestic and commercial clients. Most maid service franchises can be operated from the home and many include other cleaning services.

Management Consultant

Act as a management consultant for small- and medium-sized businesses. Offer business services to improve profits and provide counseling for companies seeking expansion. Assist companies in preparations for a sale or merger. Also assist in financial, marketing, and production planning. Some training is available, but the franchisee should have a good background in business matters from previous employment.

Pay Phones

If you are interested in working on phones, you may enjoy these franchises which have you install and service pay phones. Routes can be established in various areas, and you could work on cordless pay phone routes as well.

Personnel Agency

Many personnel agency franchises can be home based; others require an office which is accessible to clients. Such a business can be run as a one-person office specializing in domestics, housekeepers, cooks, and nannies or as a business service that refers office and management types for positions.

Picture Framing

If you have some simple handcrafting skills, you might want to consider a picture-framing franchise. Most of the time, supplies and training are offered by the franchisor. These businesses are ideal for anyone who wants to start out part-time and build a customer base before expanding operations to a retail space.

Play Programs

Play programs for parents and their children aged three months to four years can be run from your home. These programs integrate child development with parental participation and stress the importance of play. Some can be operated out of a garage or playroom that is specifically prepared for such activities. Most are usually operated at outside locations.

Property Damage Appraisers

Property damage appraisers are somewhat different from other appraisers in that they concentrate only on property that was damaged and the costs involved to repair such damage. These appraisers are sometimes called adjusters by the insurance trade. Training in direct sales, marketing, and administration is usually included as part of any franchise in this area. You often have the option of working part-time during your off hours.

Security Systems

In this franchise opportunity, you would be responsible for marketing security systems to residential and business customers. Some systems apply to both fire and burglary protection. These franchises can be operated easily from home, as long as you have space for supplies.

Telephone Answering

Telephone-answering franchises use computerized technology. Computer-assisted operators offer personalized and professional service to clients. Low overhead and recurring revenues are paramount to this home-based franchise. Additional services include mail receiving and sending.

Transportation

Offer executives and corporate clients transportation (usually luxury) to various locations. Also can be used as an airport service. The parent company provides marketing assistance to franchisees to obtain customers. Networking gives the advantage for interacting with other transportation companies.

Travel Services

Most franchisers like the franchisee to have an office that can attract walk-in trade, but some will franchise people who work from home and have a small office to service their clients.

There are general travel agencies available, which cover all forms of travel, and specialized travel agencies, which cover cruises or special trips or only corporate accounts. Check to see if a license is required and if part-time work would be appropriate to start.

Window Cleaning

Window-cleaning businesses require outside and inside work that may also require working on two-story homes. The franchisor usually provides training and equipment. So if you enjoy working out-of-doors and don't mind heights, you may want to consider a window-cleaning business.

Windshield Repair

Automobile windshield repair and scratch removal businesses require no special mechanical skills; however, the ability to work capably with hand tools is necessary. This service can be marketed to car dealers and insurance company professionals, as well as to individuals.

Gifts

People celebrate birthdays, anniversaries, weddings, graduations and other special occasions every day. With more people working longer hours, there is less time for shopping and thoughtful gift selection. Gift items prepared by you at home may be the relief these harried gift-givers are looking for. Market your gifts through the mail and at craft fairs, and place them in specialty shops and boutiques. At holiday time, gift bazaars are popular events. Find out when and where they are planned, and reserve booth space to display your products. The gifts suggested below are just a few examples of the many products you can produce or the services you can provide.

Cards and Stationery

Hand-painted stationery and greeting cards make unique and artistic gift items. Prepare several designs of prepainted stationery to be given as gifts. Take into account the various styles and designs that will be enjoyed by a wide range of people — from school-aged children to adults, both men and women. Offer a card-giving service as well. Perhaps you are good at creating caricatures or paintings that can be used as the basis of one-of-a-kind cards.

Gift Baskets

Gift baskets are always a welcome treat. These can be prepared at home and created for any theme or occasion. Keep a supply of various baskets, ribbons, decorative papers, and fillers on hand. Make baskets to fill special orders, or establish a selection of baskets in different styles and sizes. These baskets can include baked goods, toiletry items, hair accessories, stationery and writing materials, or small toys for children. The list can go on and on. If you prefer to focus on one area, advertise your product in shops, magazines, and other places that cater to the same specialty.

Gift-buying Service

If you enjoy shopping and have a knack for getting people just the right gift, you should consider a gift-buying service. In your business, you would purchase gifts for busy people who don't have the time to make unique selections. Depending on your clientele, locate wholesale outlets or select more expensive, exclusive specialty shops to do your shopping. Add in your commission, but be sure to offer competitive prices. You may want to include custom wrapping and shipping as part of your gift-buying service.

Personalized Items

Personalized and novelty items make great gifts: mugs with a name, birth date, or anniversary painted on them; a decorated cake plate to announce the birth of a baby; all sorts of children's toys — the list is endless. Anything that a person uses can be personalized; just use your imagination. Some objects can be serious and some can be created just for fun. If you are artistic, create your own designs. If you prefer working with an existing design, check the ads in entrepreneurial and small business magazines for machines that make personalized buttons, shirts, and balloons. Put together packages of personalized party items and set yourself up as a supplier of party favors.

Hobbies and Crafts

One-of-a-kind, handmade craft items are in demand today, and many people have chosen to turn their hobby and craft skills into profitable, home-based businesses. If you are artistic and like to work with your hands, why not use these talents to make extra money? As the creator of a hobby/craft product, you can choose to do your own marketing or you can use the services of an outside agency. The most common methods of distribution include mail order, retail sales, and displays at craft fairs. If you choose mail order, be sure to do your homework to determine which mailing lists will reach those customers most interested in the type of product you sell. You can prepare and send out your own brochures and order form; or your product can be included in a catalog published by a mail-order company. In such cases, the mail-order company will probably purchase a supply of your products in advance and fill orders from its inventory.

If you choose to place your product in retail stores, this can be done on consignment, or you can sell set amounts to store owners each time they request an order. For actual exhibition of your product, craft fairs are usually the best form of marketing. Be sure to have plenty of cards and brochures on hand. Because most people attending craft fairs are just out for an afternoon's fun, don't expect to sell too many of your higher-priced items. Some artisans have a special line of lower-priced products they feature at these fairs. The list of possible hobby/craft businesses could fill an entire directory of their own. Below are only a few to give you some ideas.

Antique Reproductions

Antique reproductions, ranging from clocks to sea chests, are popular items to collect. If you live in a historical area, look into the possibility of making antique reproductions. Since the country's bicentennial celebration in 1976, many towns around the United States have been celebrating similar birthdays. At local events — fairs, lectures, and parades — reproductions from the era being celebrated make wonderful sales items. Some antique stores also have a reproductions section in which your products can be put on display.

Doll Houses

Building and decorating doll houses is a popular pastime nowadays. This is an area with many facets. You can build doll houses in several styles that you finish and sell; or you can create do-it-yourself kits that your customers build themselves. In addition, you can create the small furniture, accessories, and people that go inside the houses. This type of business lends itself well to mail-order sales.

Advertise in craft/hobby magazines to build a customer base. Then prepare a direct-mail package to send to your established customer list.

Flower Baskets

Flower baskets and wreaths made with dried flowers, ribbons, and a bit of artistic flair are wonderful decorative and popular items. The wreaths can be made from discarded vines, wood, or any other base you may choose. Left in their natural color or painted to go with various decors, each wreath can be decorated differently. Baskets can be purchased or made by you, and these too can be painted and decorated to accent any home or office. Use seasonal and holiday colors to increase the selection and vibrancy of your product line.

Hand-painted Clothing

Hand-painted scarves and clothing attract attention and are very unique. Using silk scarves and clothing made from cotton or silk material, design patterns in traditional and modern styles. Flowers as well as geometric and abstract patterns are attractive.

Jewelry

Jewelry made from silver, gold, semi-precious gems, and beads are popular craft items. Focus on one particular area, silver smithing, for example, and create a unique style. Jewelry can be sold in matching sets or individually. Wear your handiwork, or have other members of your family model bracelets, necklaces, rings, and earrings. People will notice and inquire about their availability. Include styles for both men and women.

Leather Goods

Leather goods including belts, wallets, handbags, sandals, custom shoes, dog and cat collars and leashes are items that can be crafted and marketed. Model your own products and display them at craft fairs.

Plants

Plants are an interesting hobby product. Many people don't know what to do with all the cuttings and plantings they make from their favorite indoor gardens. Using pots of interesting sizes and colors, create living arrangements that can be sold at fairs or delivered as gifts. If you specialize in exotic plants, print a brochure describing their origin as well as proper care and feeding.

Potpourri

Sachets and scented pillows are gift items many women love to receive. Using dried flower petals and scented oils along with a bit of sewing know-how, you can create these fragrant products right in your home. With a little lace, ribbon, and scent you can create several themes of matching items that can be sold separately or together.

Pottery

Handcrafted bowls, cups, platters, and vases as well as decorative items are in great demand today. Usually bringing in a high price for their artistic value, these products can be sold individually or in sets. Create your own designs and product patterns in different colors. You might want to branch away from the traditional fare and create ceramic lamp bases, dolls, cups with interesting pictures and mini figurines inside, or even jewelry. There is no limit to the ways in which you can make your style unique.

Wood Crafts

Wood crafts can be produced in a basement or garage workshop. Items such as trunks, mailboxes, children's toys, doll houses, clocks, and simple furniture can be sold painted, unpainted, or designed to suit customer requirements. Wood carvings — animals, people, Indian canoes, or any other subject — also make ideal souvenirs and gifts.

Home Services

With so many people traveling for business or pleasure or devoting long hours to their jobs, there is a great demand for simple home services. This creates opportunities for home-based businesses that take care of the tasks home owners need to have done during their absence, whether for vacation or work. Begin by performing your home service jobs yourself, then, as your business grows, start a registry of people to help do the work. Many retirees or young people would like to water plants, watch houses, or walk dogs for extra money. Check out the people on your registry thoroughly. Advertise your home service business in local publications or put flyers in home supply or improvement stores. You may want to consider getting a booth at local or regional home shows as well. Home shows are a terrific way to make professional contacts as well as meet potential clients.

Attic Cleaning

Who has the time to clean and organize their attic, garage, and basement? Many homeowners put these tasks off and have trouble finding the time to do them. By offering your services for a reasonable price, you will generate some interested takers. First, help sort the valuable and practicable items from the trash items. Then, organize yard sales to generate income for your clients and charge a percentage of the sales. Find outlets that supply storage racks, shelves, and other organizing tools and design space-saving storage areas to help in organizing the area. As your customers increase, try working out discount arrangements with the suppliers of these storage materials.

Ceramic Tile Layer

Kitchens, bathrooms, around the fireplace — these are just some of the places where home owners use decorative ceramic tiles. If you are talented as a tile layer, try placing your name with tile suppliers and building contractors who may need your services. As your business grows, teach your art to apprentices who can take on some of the simpler jobs. To attract potential customers, turn your home into a showplace and take photographs which you can arrange in a portfolio to show off your work.

Chimney Sweep

Chimney sweeping is a seasonal but much needed service in many parts of the country. This service does require some training and specialized equipment. Try to attract customers by taking out a small classified ad in a local newspaper, posting flyers in shops that sell fireplace equipment or firewood, and getting a listing in your local Yellow Pages.

Closet Organizing

If you have a good sense of spacial relations and organization, you might want to consider a closet organization service. Establish modular units that fit together to create different closet combinations. Most lengths and depths of racks, shelves, and drawers can be standardized. You can provide only the organizing by handing your client a drawing, or if possible, provide the entire finished re-organized closet. Possibly team up with a carpenter if you are unable to build the finished product. There also are several franchisers available that provide this service.

Food Shopping

If you enjoy helping others, you may want to consider starting a food shopping service. Food shopping can be done for the ill, the elderly, or for busy professionals. Contact social service organizations, outpatient clinics, business organizations, and senior citizen centers to determine if there is a need for such services in your area. Your service can develop shopping lists, make food deliveries, perform the unpacking and putting away of the food. Often, elderly people contract the services of a home visitor, who stays to chat and do odd jobs around the house. You can add these or similar activities to your food shopping service.

Furniture Refinisher

Refinishing antique and not-so-old furniture is another business you can operate from your home. You will need a large space in which to work and plenty of ventilation. A truck or van may be necessary for pickup and delivery.

Handyman

Repair jobs that do not require a permit or contractor's license, such as leaky faucets, broken fences, yard work, fall into the domain of the local handyman. Gather your tools and advertise your fix-it skills by circulating flyers in your neighborhood. Since your business will require that you spend more time out of your home office than in it, a telephone answering service or machine may help to ensure that you don't miss any prospective clients who call to find out about your business.

Household Overhauls

Household overhauls as well as carpet and upholstery cleaning are valued services for the busy home owner. Advertise your services for spring and fall cleaning and sprucing up before parties and special events. Invest in some good cleaning equipment and research different methods for cleaning various fabrics. If you have a special method that no one else seems to use, advertise it! Advertise your service in local markets, repair shops, and hardware stores. If you get more requests than you can handle, hire some help and set up a referral service.

Housesitting

When people go on vacation or business trips, the last thing they want to worry about is that their empty house may be left vulnerable to burglars or pranksters, their yard and flowers may wither away, or their pipes may freeze and break.

To alleviate these and other worries, you can offer a house-sitting service where you arrange to stay at your client's home or set up a schedule to stop by and check on the house. You could even offer to take care of the family pets as a part of your services.

The start-up costs for your house-sitting service is minimal and after establishing your reliability and good reputation, you should be kept plenty busy. If you are interested in performing this type of service, check with the travel agents in your area or advertise in local publications. You could also start advertising by word-of-mouth with family, friends, and co-workers.

Interior Decorator

If you have a flare for decorating, color coordinating, and accessorizing a home, interior decorating may be for you. Interior decorators often operate from home-based offices. Investigate wholesale outlets for furniture, paint, wallpaper, carpets and home accessories, and develop contacts who will give you fast and quality service. Set up a design studio in your home complete with drawing table and materials, catalogs, and product samples. Place your name with retail stores that sell products to home owners, and advertise in local magazines and newspapers.

Lawn Care

Lawn care can be made into a year-round activity even if you live in the temperate zones. The basic tools for such a venture include a lawn mower and edging equipment. You may want to research pesticides and fertilizers so you can offer more than just a weekly or biweekly mowing service. Also, look into landscaping and design to add to your services. If you live in an area where the fall season creates the need for leaf-raking, add this to your schedule of services as well. And, if you want those year-round clients, there's always the snow on the driveways and sidewalks!

Locksmith

Lost keys, broken locks, new rentals, fear of break-ins — there are many reasons why home owners need the services of a locksmith. This is one business where the service must be provided in your customers' homes. Prepare a portable display of sample locks to suit an array of home decors. Also, be ready for those emergency calls when people find themselves locked out of their houses. Many towns require a license or registration before they allow locksmiths to practice, so be sure to check with your local governments.

Mailbox Installer and Repairs

The average life of a lonely mailbox on the side of a road is under ten years. If you are not handy at replacing it, where do you go? To the specialist who installs mailboxes or repairs them. There is a need for their service. If you are handy with your hands, fill this need. Add selling mail boxes to expand.

Plant Care

Plant care in private homes or offices is a much needed service. You may already be a budding green thumb in your own home, so make this talent profitable for you. Do some research on the feeding and watering of indoor plants. You can advertise yourself in local publications or have your name posted in nurseries and flower shops. Going from business to business and leaving your business card with the owner is a good way to drum up potential customers. Your services can include plant watering while your clients are out-of-town, general plant care and feeding, pruning and repotting, or emergency services for drooping or bug-infested plants.

Pool Cleaning

Home owners with pools in their backyards do not want to spend their leisure time cleaning the pool. What these people need are pool cleaners who come on a regular basis to vacuum and test the chlorine content of the water. Pool opening and closing at the beginning and end of the season are also important tasks.

Senior Services

There are older people who have an adequate income to pay for certain services to make their life more pleasant. Financial services such as bank deposits or withdrawal; medical services such as the filling out of necessary forms; tax services such as the gathering of information for income tax preparation are all services that can be provided for the elderly. Of course, these services can be provided to all clients but a specialty in serving the elderly may attract a special interest.

Tree Service

Tree pruning, branch cutting, removal of dead or dangerous trees, and disease treatment are services often required by home owners. For this type of business, you will need climbing spurs, a lineman's belt and rigging, ropes and cable, cutting equipment, and a truck or van capable of transporting your equipment. Many states require you to be licensed and bonded to perform these services, so be sure and check with your state licensing agency before opening your tree service business. As an additional service, get a wood chipper and offer to turn downed branches into mulch for a small fee or cut felled trees into firewood.

Mail-Order Business

A home-based, mail-order business can be very successful if you have a unique product, research your market thoroughly, and build and maintain a list of prospective buyers. One way to build a list of customers is to run keyed advertisements in newspapers and magazines. Offer an inexpensive item which can be obtained by filling in and mailing back a coupon with the remittance. People who respond to the coupon offer are likely to be prospects for future purchases.

List houses or brokers can also furnish names and addresses of potential buyers for your products, on an occupational, geographical, income-group, or other classification basis. The charge for use of a list depends on the number of names ordered and the selectivity of the list. The more selective the list, the higher the cost.

For the most part, responses from an unselective list usually run about one to two percent; responses from a selective list can go as high as five percent or more. Based on these percentages, make sure your product prices will give you a decent profit after all expenses have been deducted.

The items that you select to sell through your mail-order business depend on your interests and the market you have chosen to reach. Products can be purchased from wholesalers at reduced cost, or you can manufacture your own products. Some suggestions for mail-order businesses are listed below.

Discounted Products

You can market low-priced items through the mail that compete with similar items sold in retail outlets; however, do your research carefully before beginning this venture: It is important to research prices for items on a nationwide basis. Magazine and newspaper advertisements as well as catalog items from other suppliers are good sources for competitive pricing information.

Food Items

Food items that can be stored without refrigeration, such as candies, nuts, cookies, fruitcakes, sell well through mail-order campaigns. Make your products more desirable by shipping them in decorative canisters and tins that can be used long after the food is gone. The holidays are obvious opportunities for target mailings, but products geared for sale during other times of the year can also be a hit.

Fathers' Day and Mothers' Day, as well as end-of-the-year gifts for teachers can be popular items. A registry for shipments to children away at camp during the summer months is another idea that can attract customers.

Greeting Cards

Greeting cards, wrapping paper, ribbons and other gift decorations designed for all occasions can be popular mail-order items. Create themes in which different items are sold together as complete packages. Pricing that is lower than retail sales of similar products can make your mail-order items highly competitive.

Hobby Items

Hobbies, such as crafts and do-it-yourself activities, have produced a growing market. Read advertisements in hobby magazines before collecting your inventory to determine what products are available and sought after, and the prices at which they are being offered. Subscriber lists from these magazines can provide you with an excellent start for your direct-mail promotion.

Novelties

Novelty items or merchandise that is different from what is usually seen in retail stores are very desirable products for mail-order businesses. Imported goods, handmade items, gifts, and products created specifically for special events fall into this category. Shop around for suppliers with good prices. Since novelty products make good gifts, plan promotional mailings in time for holiday purchases.

Newspaper Delivery

If you work a full-time job but still would like to earn extra money, one good option may be the delivery of a local newspaper. All you need is a good, reliable car, preferably one with good gas mileage, and the extra hours in the morning or evening. To find out more, contact your local newspaper publisher.

Packaging and Shipping

Packaging and shipping businesses are turning up in retail spaces all over the United States; however, this is a service business you can run from your home. Add a twist — offer pickup and delivery as part of your service. You will need a van or truck and enough space to store packing materials, as well as a working countertop. You'll also have to become familiar with various shipping procedures and rates, and develop good working relationships with shipping companies.

Paper Recycling

Concern over the environment has created several business opportunities for sharp entrepreneurs. One such opportunity is in paper recycling. Check with recycling centers in your area to determine what types of paper they recycle. Payment is usually made by weight. To make your venture worthwhile, be sure you can cart the material to the center. A station wagon or van may be necessary.

Pet Care

If you like animals, there are several product or service businesses you can choose from that focus on the needs of pets and their owners. Place your name with veterinary hospitals and offices in your area and advertise in local publications. Set up a schedule and take on as many clients as you think you can handle. The businesses listed below are just a few that you can run from your home.

Breeder

Breeding dogs and cats can be a profitable business you can operate from your home. Ample kennel space, dog runs, veterinary contacts, and association with other breeders will keep you in puppies and kittens that can be sold at varying rates according to the breed.

Dog Trainer

Dog training is a service you can offer to pet owners, either in your home, or in theirs. Owners of large and small breeds alike need help with housebreaking and obedience training. Offer classes in your home for small groups. These can range from beginning to advanced instruction — distribute diplomas to owners as their dogs graduate from one step to another.

For those hard-to-handle cases, private training in the dog owner's home may be preferred.

Dog Walking

There are many dog owners who, for various reasons, cannot walk their own dogs. This service can be done before and after your full-time job, or you can create a full-time, dog-walking business. If you live in or near an apartment building that allows pets, try posting your name and phone number in the lobby or by the mailboxes. You may be surprised how many people would be relieved not to have to spend their lunch hours coming home to walk the dog. So, get to know man's best friend a little better, and the exercise and fresh air will be good for you.

Pet Feeding

While their owners are away, both dogs and cats, as well as fish and any other pets, need feeding and care. This can be done in the pet owner's home, or you can offer boarding services in your home. Invest in kennels and dog runs for your backyard. You may decide to specialize in one type of animal, cats for example, or perhaps you would rather take care of more exotic pets like baby pythons.

Pet Grooming

Claw clipping, shampooing, and brushing are services often required by pet owners. Try taking your pet grooming service on the road. Groom pets in the privacy of their owner's home, or bring the pet into your mobile "pet parlor" that is set up in the back of a van. Keep a supply of grooming products and pet accessories available, such as brushes, shampoos, collars and leashes, to sell to your clients.

Pet Product Distributor

On supermarket shelves you find all the familiar pet food products: Purina,™ Alpo,™ Mighty Dog, 9 Lives,™ Friskies,™ etc. — what you don't find are the foods for pets who require special diets. These foods are usually found only in veterinary offices and some pet supply stores. Provide these pet owners with a service and distribute the special foods their animals need — right to their doors. Ask a local veterinarian about products and manufacturers. Then contact these companies about distributorship opportunities. Once you have obtained the right to distribute a product line, prepare a brochure and take orders.

Real Estate

To act as an intermediary in real estate transactions in the United States, a license is normally required, except if you are selling your own property. There are, however, a number of other job opportunities that can be pursued from the home either as a licensed salesperson or broker, or as a contractual employee providing a specific service for a brokerage firm or a business looking for a different place of operation.

Appraiser

For a motivated individual who is capable of completing a basic real estate appraisal course, part-time work from the home can be a lucrative occupation. Banks and real estate firms are always in need of on-call appraisers who can produce evaluations of residential real estate within a few days.

Appraisal Typist

Real estate appraisers, especially independents, are always in need of typists who are familiar with standard appraisal forms. All that is needed to begin this enterprise is a list of local appraisers, a desire to succeed and , of course, a typewriter.

Commercial Real Estate

The backbone of commercial real estate is locating properties for sale or rent. Acting either as a salesperson attached to a specific firm or as an independent entrepreneur, it is possible to canvas local businesses and property owners to discover the properties that are for sale or rent. Cold calling to discover this information is an invaluable asset for the commercial real estate enterprise. Listings can either be sold outright at a fixed commission percentage or a finder's fee can be negotiated should a sale take place. Commercial real estate firms which specialize in leasing property need continual updates on the availability of space for rent. Most commercial real estate agents do not regularly canvas local businesses to discover what space is available for rent. It is possible to contract one or more of these real estate firms on a fee basis to provide such information.

Residential Real Estate

Every residential brokerage firm depends upon finding homes to sell. A valuable service that can be performed from home, either as a licensed salesperson or broker or as an independent property locator, is the discovery of available homes for sale. A local phone book is the only tool necessary to get started in this endeavor.

Self-Publisher

This is the age of information. People everywhere are looking for materials that will help them advance in their jobs, enhance their appearance, improve their athletic ability, and teach their children. With the help of personal computers and desktop publishing, enterprising people who have tuned in to this trend are supplying sought-after information with publications they produce themselves. All you need is an idea, a medium in which to present it, and a market in which to sell it. Since most print publications are sent to customers through the mail, this is also an optimum way to reach potential buyers. Research mailing lists and prepare direct-mail promotional materials. Some mail-order catalogers will also promote and distribute print materials, such as books and pamphlets. Check out royalty and licensing arrangements before placing your product with a cataloger.

Books

Books of fiction, poetry, recipes, how-to manuals, and travel guides can be written and published from your home. Write your manuscript, select and prepare artwork and photographs, set the type, lay out the pages, and you are on your way.

Directories

If you like to do research at libraries, you might want to devote yourself to directory research, either part-time or full-time, and compile resource directories for any number of subject categories. When complete, these can be self-published or sold to directory publishers.

Newsletters

Newsletters provide fast-breaking information to their subscribers. They can be published to offer informational news to local or larger audiences. Usually published with no more than two print colors and containing less than 16 pages, newsletters are a popular format for home-based publishing businesses.

Sewing Alterations

Take seams in; let them out — alterations from simple changes in hem lines to size changes of complete outfits can be done from your home. Offer emergency repair services for those jobs that must be done right away: the bridesmaid's dress that doesn't fit the day before the wedding; or the broken zipper on the slacks of the grey flannel, three-piece suit that must be worn to tomorrow's job interview.

Advertise your service in local publications, including your local Yellow Pages. Even though most dry cleaning services have an on-site tailor, give them your name for those emergency repairs they cannot handle. Department stores with clothing departments and small dress shops and boutiques may also require your services.

Travel Agent

Make hotel reservations, transportation arrangements, and discount fares your specialty. Directories of hotels, motels, and bed and breakfast inns, as well as local and international directories for both ground and air transportation can help you get started.

Begin by specializing in a certain area of the world, such as Mexico or Great Britain, or perhaps you can create a historic sites itinerary for people who want to travel in a particular part of the United States. Keep your eyes open for discount fares and accommodation rates. Place your name with local tourist information bureaus, and advertise in local publications.

Videotaping

Do you own a video camera and recorder? If so, have you considered opening your own on-location videotaping business? At one time, photographers were invited to capture special events, such as weddings and graduations, on film but now the new person on the scene is the videographer. With so many people owning consumer videotape recorders, the trend is to watch the special events on television, rather than browsing through pages of still pictures. This is also true of school yearbooks, which are now becoming popular as video yearbooks. Costs of consumer-grade editing equipment have also been dropping and you can offer professional-quality videos at low prices. Advertise in local publications and place your name with organizations sponsoring special events. It also helps to get the names of a few good tape duplicators who can supply you with low-cost copies of your tapes as well as the names of potential customers. Having completed this tour of business ideas, hopefully you have discovered a business area you are particularly interested in. For your convenience, a list of additional resources that detail some of these business ideas is located in Appendix D. If a business idea you would like to investigate doesn't have an additional resource listed, check with your local library for magazine articles available on the subject.

Mile Post

Take your time and research any business opportunity you are interested in pursuing. This extra effort will pay off in the long run because you will be more informed and prepared.

Chapter
9

Set Your Sights on Success

In the preceding chapters, ideas and information were presented on how to select and start a business from your home; the types of businesses you can start; and the varied ways you can implement them. At this point, after having read each chapter carefully, you should have a clear idea as to whether you would be most happy and apt to succeed in a service or product business; as the producer and marketer of your own product or the distributor of a product created by someone else; in a franchise or a self-started operation; and working on your new venture on a full-time or part-time basis.

A major ingredient to being successful in any business venture is to enjoy what you are doing. You should have the necessary skills to pursue a particular business and the capital investment for that business. Your enjoyment while pursuing your new venture as well as how the business fits with your lifestyle are important factors that contribute to your eventual success.

As you proceed, keep in mind that any new business requires the dedication of its owner. Behind all those so-called overnight successes we hear about from time to time are stories of hard work. No one gets by without persisting and persevering. If you like what you are doing, think of how much easier it will be to get over any obstacles that may get in your way.

Define Your Objectives

With your business idea in mind and the determination to see your venture through, don't overlook the area you are about to enter. Be sure to define your business thoroughly. What product or service will your business offer? To what geographical area will you sell? What are your prices? How much space will you need for your business? What investment is required? Do you have a marketing plan? Does your business have potential future growth? These are important considerations that must be made before you begin.

Gather Information and Support

As you prepare to operate your new business, gather information about your competition and be ready to give your business the competitive push it may need to succeed in a market in which there are existing players. If you have your heart set on one particular product, a wooden rocking horse for example, but a competitor has already placed his horses on consignment in all the toy stores in your area, you may need to find another method to sell your product — or perhaps, your best option may be to create a different product.

It is better to find out about changes you need to plan for before you invest time and money, rather than after. Talk with other business owners who have entered fields similar to yours. Listen carefully to what they have to say. A word from the wise can keep you from making costly mistakes.

Gather as much support around you as you can. Because you will be working from home, the positive attitudes of family members toward your new business can help to carry you through the tough first phase of initiation as you begin to get your business rolling — a strong cheering section never hurt anyone.

Observe Government Regulations

The importance of finding out about government regulations that might affect the operation of your new business cannot be overstated. You don't want to initiate your company only to find out that you have to shut down until you can resume operations legally.

Many businesses are required to obtain a license or special permit prior to conducting business. Commercial and residential zoning regulations are also important for home-based business owners, especially if you intend to have customers coming and going from your premises throughout an average work day.

No matter what business you choose, find out what regulations affect you, then be sure to implement whatever actions may be necessary to ensure the legal operation of your new business. Your business survival may depend on it.

Let Growth Increase Your Chances for Success

As your business grows and develops, don't be afraid to look for new ways of approaching your clients and customers. You may be rolling right along making ends meet, but if you want growth, you must be able to adapt to changes necessary to make your business expand. Give your venture a shot in the arm with new marketing ideas, expanded new products or services, or delegating responsibility to others in order to allow your business to grow. In order to get more out of your business, you must be willing to take additional risks. To coin a popular phrase: "Nothing ventured, nothing gained."

Final Thought

As the owner of a new home business, you are starting an adventure. Take it slowly and carefully as you progress down the road toward success. Above all, as your dream becomes a reality, don't forget that you are what makes it happen.

Appendix A

Associations & Organizations

This appendix lists several types of organizations and associations that you may find of particular interest as a prospective or new home business owner. This listing includes organizations covering business in general, specific professions, and various trade industries. To find out what each organization and association offers, write to the appropriate address. In some instances, you can call to request more information.

Aerobics and Fitness Association
15250 Ventura Boulevard, Suite 200
Sherman Oaks, CA 91403
(818) 905-0040

American Accounting Association
5717 Bessie Drive
Sarasota, FL 34233
(941) 921-7747

American Advertising Federation
1101 Vermont Avenue, Suite 500
Washington, DC 20005
(202) 898-0089

American Bed and Breakfast Association
P.O. Box 1387
Midlothian, VA 23113
(804) 379-2222

American Boarding Kennel Association
4575 Galley Road, Suite 400A
Colorado Springs, CO 80915
(719) 591-1113

The American Craft Council
21 South Eltings Corner Road
Highland, NY 12528
(914) 883-6100

American Home Sewing Association
1375 Broadway
New York, NY 10018
(212) 302-2150

American Kennel Club
51 Madison Avenue
New York, NY 10010
(212) 696-8234

American Marketing Association
60 East 42nd Street, Suite 1765
New York, NY 10165

American Rabbit Breeder's Association
P.O. Box 426
Bloomington, IL 61702
(309) 827-6623

American Society of Home Inspectors
85 West Algonquin Road, Suite 360
Arlington Heights, IL 60005-4423
(708) 290-1919

American Welding Society
550 NW LeJeune Road
Miami, FL 33126
(305) 443-9353

Associated Landscape Contractors of America
12200 Sunrise Valley Drive, Suite 15
Reston, VA 22091
(703) 620-6363

Bed and Breakfast League
Sweet Dreams and Toast
P.O. Box 9490
Washington, DC 20016
(202) 363-7767

Better Lawn and Turf Institute
P.O. Box 108
Pleasant Hill, TN 38578
(615) 277-3722

Center for Entrepreneurial Management
180 Varrack Street, 17th Floor
New York, NY 10014
(212) 633-0060

Child Care Information Exchange
P.O. Box 2890
Redmond, WA 98073-2890
(206) 883-9394

Direct Marketing Association
120 Avenue of the Americas
New York, NY 10036-8096
(212) 768-7277

Direct Selling Association
1666 K Street NW, Suite 1010
Washington, DC 20006-2808
(202) 293-5760

Embroiderer's Guild of America
335 West Broadway, Suite 100
Louisville, KY 40202
(502) 589-6956

Home Business Institute
P.O. Box 301
White Plains, NY 10605
(914) 946-6600

Home Office Association of America
909 Third Avenue, Suite 990
New York, NY 10022

Independent Computer Consultants Association
933 Gardenview Office Parkway
St. Louis, MO 63141
(314) 997-4633
(800) 438-4222

International Franchise Association
1350 New York Avenue, NW, Suite 900
Washington, DC 20005
(202) 628-8000

Juvenile Product Manufacturer's Association
Two Greentree Center, Suite 225
P.O. Box 955
Marlton, NJ 08053
(609) 231-8500

Mail Order Association of America
Patton Boggs, LLP
2550 M Street, NW, 9th Floor
Washington, DC 20037
(202) 457-6000

National Association for the Cottage Industry
P.O. Box 14850
Chicago, IL 60614
(312) 472-8116

National Association for the Self-Employed (NASE)
1023 15th Street, NW, Suite 1200
Washington, DC 20005-2600
(800) 232-6275

National Association of Home-Based Businesses
P.O. Box 30220
Baltimore, MD 21270
(301) 363-3698

National Association of Realtors
700 11th Street, NW
Washington, DC 20001-4507
(202) 383-1000

National Bed and Breakfast Association
P.O. Box 332
Norwalk, CT 06852
(203) 847-0469

National Business Association
P.O. Box 700728
Dallas, TX 75287
(800) 456-0440

National Business Owners Association
1033 North Fairfax Street, Suite 402
Alexandria, VA 22314-1540
(703) 838-2850

National Chimney Sweep Guild
16021 Industrial Drive, Suite 8
Gaithersburg, MD 20877
(301) 963-5600

National Council on the Aging
National Institute of Adult Day Care
409 3rd Street, Suite 200
Washington, DC 20024
(202) 479-1200

National Dog Groomers Association of America
P.O. Box 101
Clark, PA 16113
(412) 962-2711

**National Federation of
 Independent Business (NFIB)**
600 Maryland Avenue, SW, Suite 700
Washington, DC 20024
(202) 554-9000

National Small Business United
1156 15th Street, NW, Suite 1100
Washington, DC 20005-1711
(202) 293-8830

Newsletter Publishers Association
1401 Wilson Boulevard, Suite 207
Arlington, VA 22209
(703) 527-2333

NRI Schools
**McGraw-Hill Continuing Education
 Center**
4401 Connecticut Avenue, NW
Washington, DC 20008
(202) 244-1600

Small Business Institute National Center
University of Central Arkansas
College of Business
UCA P.O. Box 5018
Conway, AR 72032
(501) 450-5300

Small Business Service Bureau
554 Main Street
P.O. Box 1441
Worcester, MA 01615-0014
(508) 756-3513

Promotional Products Association International
3125 Skyway Circle, North
Irving, TX 75038-3526
(214) 252-0404

U.S. Chamber of Commerce
Small Business Center
1615 H Street, NW
Washington, DC 20062
(202) 463-5503

U.S. Patent and Trademark Office
U.S. Department of Commerce
Washington, DC 20231
(703) 308-0975

U.S. Small Business Administration
409 3rd Street, SW, Suite 4000
Washington, DC 20416
(202) 205-6770

Appendix B

General Business Publications

Here are some publications that provide continuing information on business in general and small businesses in particular. There are also a number of specialized publications, such as resource directories, you may find particularly helpful. Many of these publications can be located through your local library or you can contact the publishers at the addresses below.

American Business Directories
American Business Directories, Inc.
5711 South 86th Circle
P.O. Box 27347
Omaha, NE 68127
(402) 593-4600
(402) 331-5105 (FAX)

Yellow Pages information for more than 1,300 types of businesses across the U.S.

Assets Protection
Territorial Imperative, Inc.
P.O. Box 5323
Madison, WI 53705-0323
(608) 271-6768

Ways to protect assets from fraud, abuse, and waste.

Associations Yellow Book
Monitor Publishing Co.
104 5th Avenue 2nd Floor, 1000
New York, NY 10011
(212) 627-4140
(212) 645-0931 (FAX)

Comprehensive directory for more than 30,000 officers, managers, and more of major trade and professional organizations in the U.S.

AT&T Toll-Free 800 Directory – Business Edition
AT&T Communications
(800) 422-8793
(800) 522-8793 (FAX)

Toll-free numbers for business-to-business calling.

Barter News
P.O. Box 3024
Mission Viejo, CA 92690-1024
(714) 831-0607

Ways to use barter as a business tool.

Bond's Franchise Guide
The Oasis Press
300 North Valley Drive
Grants Pass, OR 97526
(800) 228-2275

Lists 1,200 franchise profiles.

The Business Environmental Handbook
The Oasis Press
300 North Valley Drive
Grants Pass, OR 97526
(800) 228-2275

How businesses can profit by being environmentally aware.

Business Owner
Thomas Publications Inc.
383 South Broadway
Hicksville, NY 11801-5081
(516) 681-2111

Issues and articles on being a business owner.

Business Start-Ups
Entrepreneur Media
2392 Morse Avenue
Irvine, CA 92714
(800) 274-8333

Issues and articles written for start-up companies.

Complete Book of Business Forms
The Oasis Press
300 North Valley Drive
Grants Pass, OR 97526
(800) 228-2275

Hundreds of reproducible forms for a wide range of business needs and activities.

Cottage Connection
National Association for the Cottage Industry
P.O. Box 14850
Chicago, IL 60614-0850
(312) 472-8116

Information and updates on business and government for home business owners.

Entrepreneur Magazine
**Entrepreneur Magazine's Guide to
  Franchise & Business Opportunities**
The Entrepreneur Group
2392 Morse Avenue
Irvine, CA 92714-6234
(714) 261-2325
(714) 755-4211 (FAX)

Research and start-up details on small businesses.

Extra Income
Business Concepts Inc.
734 Monte Drive
Santa Barbara, CA 93105
(805) 569-1363

How to start a business, business opportunities for retirees, and more.

Family Business
MLR Publishing Co.
229 South 18th Street, 3rd Floor
Philadelphia, PA 19103
(215) 790-7000

General issues and information for family-run businesses.

Family Business Report
Independent Business Institute
3234 South Cleve-Mass Road
Norton, OH 44203
(330) 825-8258

Planning for privately owned businesses.

Family Business Review
Jossey-Bass Publishers
350 Sansome Street, 5th Floor
San Francisco, CA 94104
(415) 433-1740
Ideas and strategies for family-run businesses.

Franchise Annual Directory
Info Press
P.O. Box 550
728 Center Street
Lewiston, NY 14092-0550
(716) 754-4669
Listings of franchises.

Home Office Computing Magazine
411 Lafayette, 4th Floor
New York, NY 10003
(212) 505-4241
Monthly publication for home office owner.

Inc. Magazine
30 Commercial Wharf
Boston, MA 02110
(800) 234-0990
Valuable resource for start-up and growing companies.

Independent Business
National Federation of Independent Business (NFIB)
125 Auburn Court, Suite 100
Thousand Oaks, CA 91362-3617
(805) 496-6156
NFIB membership magazine covering a variety of
features and issues pertaining to small businesses.

Inside Home Business
Home Business Institute
P.O. Box 301
White Plains, NY 10605
(888) DIAL-HBI
Home business newsletter.

Journal of Private Enterprise
Association of Private Enterprise Education
University of Tennessee
Martin, TN 38238-5015
(901) 587-7208

**National Trade and Professional Associations
 of the United States**
Columbia Books, Inc.
1212 New York Avenue, NW, Suite 330
Washington, DC 20005
(202) 898-0662

Nation's Business
U.S. Chamber of Commerce
1615 H Street, NW
Washington, DC 20062-2000
(202) 463-5650

News and information for businesses in general.

**Safety Law Compliance Manual for
  California Businesses**
The Oasis Press
300 North Valley Drive
Grants Pass, OR 97526
(800) 228-2275

Compliance with Senate Bill 198.

SBIC Digest
U.S. Small Business Administration
409 3rd Street, SW
Washington, DC 20416-0001
(202) 205-6600
(800) 827-5722 (outside DC)

Information of interest to SBIC/MESBIC management and venture capital industry.

Small Business America
National Association for the Self-Employed, Inc.
1023 15th Street, NW, Suite 1200
Washington, DC 20005-2600
(800) 232-6275

Monthly NASE member newsletter.

Small Business Journal
Nason & Associates
P.O. Box 8204
Asheville, NC 28814-8204
(704) 298-1322

General information for small businesses.

Small Business Service Bureau Bulletin
Small Business Service Bureau
554 Main Street
P.O. Box 15014
Worcester, MA 01615-0014
(508) 756-3513

Small business legislation, benefits, services and more.

Small Business — USA
National Small Business United
1156 15th Street, NW, Suite 1100
Washington, DC 20005
(202) 293-8830

For members of the National Small Business Association describing its activities in Washington, D.C.

Success Magazine
Lane Communications
230 Park Avenue
New York, NY 10169
(212) 551-9500

Strategies for today's entrepreneurs.

Tradeshow 200
Cahners Publishing Co.
5700 Wilshire Boulevard, Suite 120
Los Angeles, CA 90036
(213) 965-5300

Information on the 200 largest trade shows.

Your Company
American Express Publishing Company
1271 Avenue of Americas
New York, NY 10020-1393

Helpful tips for the American Express cardholder.

Appendix C

Small Business Development Center State Offices

Small Business Development Centers (SBDCs) are sponsored by the U.S. Small Business Administration (SBA) in partnership with state and local governments, the educational community, and the private sector. SBDCs provide help to prospective, new, and existing businesses in the following areas:

Counseling. Free counseling from a qualified staff of professionals in your area can advise you on the type of help you need in marketing, financing and financial analysis, operations, business planning, and general management.

Training and Continuing Education. Low cost seminars and workshops, statewide conferences, and co-ventured programs (with other institutions) focus on such topics as loan packaging, sales management, recordkeeping and taxes, computers, exporting, women in business, and procurement.

Information and Referral. The SBDCs can provide information or refer you to other agencies (civic, state, or federal) or private organizations that have the resources or technical information a business needs. A variety of publications and resource materials are also available.

Every state has an SBDC network, and nearly all SBDCs are located on university and community college campuses. They are an excellent resource for any home business owner. To find the SBDC nearest you, call your state's main SBDC office listed on the following pages.

Alabama

SBDC: University of Alabama at Birmingham
1717 11th Avenue, South, Suite 419
Birmingham, AL 35294-4410
(205) 934-7260

Alaska

SBDC: University of Alaska at Anchorage
430 West Seventh Avenue, Suite 110
Anchorage, AK 99501
(907) 274-7232
(800) 478-7232 (outside Anchorage)

Arizona

SBDC: Maricopa Community College
2411 West 14th Street, Suite 132
Tempe, AZ 85281-6941
(602) 731-8720

Arkansas

SBDC: University of Arkansas at Little Rock
100 South Main Street, Suite 401
Little Rock, AR 72201
(501) 324-9043

California

SBDC: California Trade & Commerce Agency
801 K Street, Suite 1700
Sacramento, CA 95814
(916) 324-5068

Colorado

SBDC: Office of Business Development
1625 Broadway, Suite 1710
Denver, CO 80202
(303) 892-3809

Connecticut

SBDC: University of Connecticut
2 Bourn Place, U-94
Storrs, CT 06269-5094
(203) 486-4135

Delaware

SBDC: University of Delaware
Purnell Hall, Suite 005
Newark, DE 19716
(302) 831-1555

District of Columbia

SBDC: Howard University
2600 Sixth Street, NW, Room 125
Washington, DC 20059
(202) 806-1550

Florida

SBDC: University of West Florida
Downtown Center
19 West Garden Street, Suite 300
Pensacola, FL 32501
(904) 444-2060

Georgia

SBDC: University of Georgia
Chicopee Complex
1180 East Broad Street
Athens, GA 30602-5412
(706) 542-6762

Hawaii

SBDC: Hawaii State Office
200 West Kawili Street
Hilo, HI 96720-4091
(808) 974-7515

Idaho

SBDC: Boise State University
1910 University Drive
Boise, ID 83725
(208) 385-3875
(800) 225-3815 (in Idaho)

Illinois

SBDC: Department of Commerce &
  Community Affairs
620 East Adams Street
Springfield, IL 62701
(217) 524-5856

Indiana

SBDC: Indiana Network Lead Center
Economic Development Council
One North Capitol, Suite 420
Indianapolis, IN 46204
(317) 264-6871

Iowa

SBDC: Iowa State University
137 Lynn Avenue
Ames, IA 50014-7126
(515) 292-6351

Kansas

SBDC: State Office (Main Office)
214 SW 6th Street, Suite 205
Topeka, KS 66603
(913) 296-6514

Kentucky

SBDC: University of Kentucky
Gatton Business College
Center for Entrepreneurship
Lexington, KY 40506-0034
(606) 257-7668

Louisiana

SBDC: Northeast Louisiana University
College of Business Administration 2-57
Monroe, LA 71209-6435
(318) 342-5506

Maine

SBDC: University of Southern Maine
96 Falmouth Street
USM P.O. Box 9300
Portland, ME 04104-9300
(207) 780-4949

Maryland

SBDC: University of Maryland
7100 Baltimore Avenue, Suite 401
College Park, MD 20740-3627
(301) 403-8300

Massachusetts

SBDC: University of Massachusetts – Amherst
205 School of Management
Amherst, MA 01003
(413) 545-6301

Michigan

SBDC: Wayne State University
2727 Second Avenue, Suite 107
Detroit, MI 48201
(313) 964-1798

Minnesota

SBDC: Minnesota Department of Trade &
  Economic Development
500 Metro Square
121 7th Place, East
St. Paul, MN 55101-2146
(612) 297-5770
(800) 657-3501

Mississippi

Mississippi Small Business Development Center
Old Chemistry Building, Suite 216
University, MS 38677
(601) 232-5001

Missouri

SBDC: University of Missouri — Columbia
300 University Place
Columbia, MO 65211
(573) 882-0344

Montana

SBDC: Montana Department of Commerce
Economic Development Division
1424 9th Avenue
Helena, MT 59620
(406) 444-4780

Nebraska

Nebraska Business Development Center
1313 Farnam-on-the-Mall, Suite 132
Omaha, NE 68182
(402) 595-2381

Nevada

SBDC: University of Nevada — Reno
Mail Stop 032
1664 North Virginia Street
Reno, NV 89557-0100
(702) 784-1717

New Hampshire

SBDC: University of New Hampshire
108 McConnell Hall
Durham, NH 03824-3593
(603) 862-2200

New Jersey

SBDC: University Heights
School of Management
180 University Avenue
Newark, NJ 07102
(201) 648-5950

New Mexico

SBDC: Santa Fe Community College
P.O. Box 4187
Santa Fe, NM 87502-4187
(505) 438-1362

New York

SBDC: State University of New York
State U Plaza, S527
Albany, NY 12246
(518) 443-5398
(800) 732-SBDC (in New York State)

North Carolina

SBTDC: Headquarters
333 Fayetteville Street Mall, Suite 1150
Raleigh, NC 27601
(919) 715-7272

North Dakota

SBDC: Lead Center
P.O. Box 7308
Grand Forks, ND 58202-7308
(701) 777-3700

Ohio

SBDC: Central Ohio
Columbus Chamber of Commerce
37 North High Street
Columbus, OH 43215
(614) 225-6910

Oklahoma

SBDC: Southeastern Oklahoma State University
517 University
Durant, OK 74701
(800) 522-6154

Oregon

OSBDC: Network Office
44 West Broadway, Suite 501
Eugene, OR 97401-3021
(541) 726-2250

Pennsylvania

SBDC: University of Pennsylvania State Office
Vance Hall, 4th Floor
3733 Spruce Street
Philadelphia, PA 19104-6374
(215) 898-1219

Rhode Island

SBDC: Bryant College
1150 Douglas Pike
Smithfield, RI 02917-1284
(401) 232-6111

South Carolina
SBDC: University of South Carolina
College of Business Administration
Columbia, SC 29208
(803) 777-4907

South Dakota
SBDC: University of South Dakota
School of Business
414 East Clark Street
Vermillion, SD 57069
(605) 677-5498

Tennessee
SBDC: University of Memphis
South Campus, Getwell Road, Building 1
Memphis, TN 38152
(901) 678-2500

Texas
SBDC: North Texas
1402 Corinth Street
Dallas, TX 75215
(214) 860-5835

Texas (continued)
SBDC: Houston — Region Main Office
University of Houston
1100 Louisiana, Suite 500
Houston, TX 77002
(713) 752-8444

SBDC: South Texas Border
UTSA Downtown — Cypress Tower
1222 North Main Street, Suite 450
San Antonio, TX 78212
(210) 458-2450

SBDC: Texas Tech University
2579 South Loop 289, Suite 210
Lubbuck, TX 79423
(806) 745-3973

Utah
SBDC: Salt Lake Community College
8811 South 700 East
Sandy, UT 84070
(801) 255-5878

Vermont

SBDC: Vermont State Office
Vermont Technical College
P.O. Box 422
Randolph, VT 05060-0422
(802) 728-9101

Virginia

SBDC: Virginia
901 East Byrd Street, Suite 1800
Richmond, VA 23219
(804) 371-8253

Washington

SBDC: Washington State University
P.O. Box 644851
501 Johnson Tower
Pullman, WA 99164-4851
(509) 335-1576

West Virginia

SBDC: West Virginia
950 Kanawha Boulevard, East
Charleston, WV 25301
(304) 558-2960

Wisconsin

SBDC: Wisconsin Headquarters
432 North Lake Street, Suite 423
Madison, WI 53706
(608) 263-7794

Wyoming

SBDC: Wyoming State Office
P.O. Box 3922
Laramie, WY 82071-3922
(307) 766-3505

Appendix D

Chapter-specific Resources

This appendix features additional resource materials for chapters 2–8. These resources provide you with the opportunity to obtain more comprehensive or related information on the topics discussed in each chapter. The publishers' addresses, and phone numbers when available, are provided.

Chapter 2

The Entrepreneur's Complete Self-Assessment Guide
Self-Counsel Press Inc.
1704 North State Street
Bellingham, WA 98225
(800) 663-3007

A step-by-step guide for assessing suitability and putting ideas into action.

Moonlighting: Earning a Second Income at Home
The Oasis Press
300 North Valley Drive
Grants Pass, OR 97526
(800) 228-2275

A detailed how-to for part-time entrepreneurs.

My Own Boss
CAE Consultants Inc.
41 Travers Avenue
Yonkers, NY 10705-1648
(914) 963-3695

For people who want to start their own businesses.

Which Business?
The Oasis Press
300 North Valley Drive
Grants Pass, OR 97526
(800) 228-2275

Help in selecting your new venture.

Chapter 3

Develop & Market Your Creative Ideas
The Oasis Press
300 North Valley Drive
Grants Pass, OR 97526
(800) 228-2275

A step-by-step guide to successfully bringing new ideas to the marketplace.

Income Opportunities Magazine
1555 Broadway, Suite 600
New York, NY 10036
(212) 642-0600

Ideas for earning money at home.

New Inventions WORLD
Lott Publishing Co.
P.O. Box 710
Santa Monica, CA 90406-1107
(213) 397-4217

Covers the field of new inventions.

Small Business Opportunities
Harris Publications Inc.
1115 Broadway, 8th Floor
New York, NY 10010-2897
(212) 807-7100

Information on business opportunities and ideas.

Chapter 4

The Buyer's Guide to Business Insurance
The Oasis Press
300 North Valley Drive
Grants Pass, OR 97526
(800) 228-2275

Helps businesses combat today's rising insurance costs.

Collection Techniques for a Small Business
The Oasis Press
300 North Valley Drive
Grants Pass, OR 97526
(800) 228-2275

How to reduce bad debts and collect what you are owed.

Chapter 4 (continued)

Findex: The Directory of Market Research Reports, Studies & Surveys

Cambridge Scientific Abstracts
7200 Wisconsin Avenue, Suite 601
Bethesda, MD 20814-4823
(301) 961-6700
(301) 961-6720 (FAX)

Directory of commercially available market research reports and studies.

Friendship Marketing

The Oasis Press
300 North Valley Drive
Grants Pass, OR 97526
(800) 228-2275

Shows how to build profitable and worthwhile relationships.

Know Your Market

The Oasis Press
300 North Valley Drive
Grants Pass, OR 97526
(800) 228-2275

How to conduct market research.

Start Your Business

The Oasis Press
300 North Valley Drive
Grants Pass, OR 97526
(800) 228-2275

A learning guide to start a business.

Starting and Operating a Business series

The Oasis Press
300 North Valley Drive
Grants Pass, OR 97526
(800) 228-2275

Complete, easy-to-understand guide to the federal and state laws and regulations that your business must know about and follow, plus basic business pointers. Request the edition for your state.

The Successful Business Plan: Secrets & Strategies

The Oasis Press
300 North Valley Drive
Grants Pass, OR 97526
(800) 228-2275

Start-to-finish guide to creating a successful business plan, with personal tips from bankers, venture capitalists, and business leaders. Includes sample business plan and easy worksheets.

Chapter 5

Business Franchise Guide
Commerce Clearing House Inc.
4025 West Peterson Avenue
Chicago, IL 60646-6085
(312) 583-8500

Rules and developments affecting franchising.

Distributor's & Wholesaler's Advisor
Alexander Research & Communications, Inc.
215 Park Avenue South, Suite 1301
New York, NY 10003
(212) 228-0246

Franchise Bible: A Comprehensive Guide
The Oasis Press
300 North Valley Drive
Grants Pass, OR 97526
(800) 228-2275

Complete information on how to acquire a franchise and how to franchise a business.

Ideas & Solutions
Gibbs Publishing Co.
P.O. Box 600927
North Miami Beach, FL 33160-0927
(305) 947-4393

For businesses, products, and services.

Journal of Direct Marketing
John Wiley & Sons Inc.
605 3rd Avenue
New York, NY 10158-0012
(212) 850-6000

Scholarly publication for direct marketing.

Mail Order Legal Guide
The Oasis Press
300 North Valley Drive
Grants Pass, OR 97526
(800) 228-2275

A guide to federal, state, and local mail order laws.

Chapter 5 (continued)

Marketing Mastery
The Oasis Press
300 North Valley Drive
Grants Pass, OR 97526
(800) 228-2275

A step-by-step guide to creating and implementing a marketing plan.

Successful Network Marketing
The Oasis Press
300 North Valley Drive
Grants Pass, OR 97526
(800) 228-2275

Shows how network marketing fits home based business.

TargetSmart
The Oasis Press
300 North Valley Drive
Grants Pass, OR 97526
(800) 228-2275

Explains how to implement and develop database marketing.

Chapter 6

A Company Policy and Personnel Workbook
The Oasis Press
300 North Valley Drive
Grants Pass, OR 97526
(800) 228-2275

A practical, easy-to-use guide for developing a company policy manual. Includes over 20 personnel forms.

The Essential Corporation Handbook
The Oasis Press
300 North Valley Drive
Grants Pass, OR 97526
(800) 228-2275

Explanations of the principles, rules, and documents crucial to corporate maintenance and formation.

The Essential Limited Liability Company Handbook
The Oasis Press
300 North Valley Drive
Grants Pass, OR 97526
(800) 228-2275

Assists you in forming an LLC or converting an existing business.

Chapter 6 (continued)

Financial Management Techniques for Small Business

The Oasis Press
300 North Valley Drive
Grants Pass, OR 97526
(800) 228-2275

How to learn and apply financial basics.

Financing Your Small Business

The Oasis Press
300 North Valley Drive
Grants Pass, OR 97526
(800) 228-2275

How to gain the benefits of debt while minimizing risks.

Handbook for Small Business

Superintendent of Documents
U.S. Government Printing Office
Washington, DC 20402-0001
(202) 512-1800

Descriptions of federal programs that assist small businesses; where to get more information.

The Insider's Guide To Small Business Loans

The Oasis Press
300 North Valley Drive
Grants Pass, OR 97526
(800) 228-2275

How to prepare a winning loan proposal.

Network News

Network of Small Businesses
5420 Mayfield Road, Suite 205
Lyndhurst, OH 44124
(216) 442-5600

Financial assistance for new or expanding businesses.

Surviving and Prospering in a Business Partnership

The Oasis Press
300 North Valley Drive
Grants Pass, OR 97526
(800) 228-2275

A guide to forming, managing, and dissolving business partnerships.

Chapter 6 (continued)

Write Your Own Business Contracts
The Oasis Press
300 North Valley Drive
Grants Pass, OR 97526
(800) 228-2275

The do's and don'ts of writing legal contracts and tips on working with your attorney.

Chapter 7

Guide to Free Tax Services, Publication 910
Tax Guide for Small Business, Publication 334
Internal Revenue Service
Washington, DC 20403
(800) 829-3676

Free publications that assist you in dealing with federal tax laws.

Profit-Building Strategies for Business Owners
(Tax Update)
TRR Publishing Co. Inc.
81 Montgomery Street
Scarsdale, NY 10583
(914) 472-0366

Ideas to help small businesses be more successful.

The Small Business Insider's Guide to Bankers
The Oasis Press
300 North Valley Drive
Grants Pass, OR 97526
(800) 228-2275

Guide to building strong banking relationship.

Top Tax Saving Ideas for Today's Small Business
The Oasis Press
300 North Valley Drive
Grants Pass, OR 97526
(800) 228-2275

Summary of available tax breaks in today's "reform" tax environment.

Chapter 8

A Parent's Guide to Day Care
U.S. Department of Health and Human Services
Washington, DC 20201
(202) 619-0257

Chapter 8 (continued)

Franchise Opportunities Guide
(IFA Membership Directory)
International Franchise Association (IFA)
1350 New York Avenue, NW, Suite 900
Washington, D.C. 20005
(202) 628-8000
(800) 543-1038

Listing of world's leading franchise companies.

Franchising Advisor
Shepard's/McGraw-Hill Inc.
555 Middle Creek Parkway
Colorado Springs, CO 80935-3530
(800) 899-6000

Key elements of a successful franchising system.

Franchising in the U.S.
Self-Counsel Press Inc.
1704 North State Street
Bellingham, WA 98225
(800) 663-3007

Discusses factors for finding the right type of franchise for you.

Index

From The Oasis Press®
The Leading Publisher of Small Business Information.

At The Oasis Press® we take pride in helping you and two million other businesses grow.

We hope that *Home Business Made Easy* has helped you move closer to a successful business start-up at home, but we also want you to know that The Oasis Press® is your resource for other business issues you may encounter. On the following pages, we offer a brief sampling of The Successful Business Library — books and software that will help you solve your day-to-day business questions as well as prepare you for unexpected problems your business may be facing down the road. We offer up-to-date and practical business solutions, which are easy to use and understand. Call for a complete catalog or let our knowledgeable sales representatives point you in the right direction.

Your input means a lot to us — we hope to hear from you!

Choose from the following related titles to help your business grow.

The Insider's Guide to Small Business Loans

Essential for the small business operator in search of capital, this helpful, hands-on guide simplifies the loan application process as never before. The Insider's Guide to Small Business Loans is an easy-to-follow road map designed to help you cut through the red tape and show you how to prepare a successful loan application.

Available in either paperback or binder formats.
Paperback $19.95 (ISBN 1-55571-373-4)
3-Ring Binder $29.95 (ISBN 1-55571-378-5)

The Oasis Press® offers
books and software that will save your time and money!

Updated Edition!

Business Owner's Guide to Accounting & Bookkeeping

Updated and released the fall of 1997! This guide makes understanding the economics of your business simple. Explains the basic accounting principles that relate to any business. Step-by-step instructions for generating accounting statements and interpreting them, spotting errors, and recognizing warning signs. Discusses how creditors view financial statements too.

Available in paperback!
Paperback $19.95 (ISBN 1-55571-381-5)

Top Tax Saving Ideas for Today's Small Business

An extensive summary of every imaginable tax break that is still available in today's "reform" tax environment. The current and helpful resource goes beyond most tax guides on the market that focuses on the tax season only., instead it provides readers with year-round strategies to lower taxes and avoid common pitfalls. Identifies a wide assortment of tax deduction, fringe benefits, and tax deferrals. Includes a simplified checklist of recent tax law changes with an emphasis on tax breaks.

Available in paperback!
Paperback $16.95 (ISBN 1-55571-343-2)

New from The Oasis Press®
A complete guide to easily assist you in starting up your own business through today's complex business environment.

SmartStart Your (State) Business

There has never been a better time to start a small business. According to a recent study by the Entrepreneurial Research Consortium, one out of three U.S. households has someone who is involved in a small business startup. With statistics like these, the odds seem to be in your favor... until you start dealing with the many regulations, laws, and financial requirements placed on twenty-first century business owners.

SmartStart Your (State) Business goes a step beyond other business how-to books and provides you with:

• Quick reference to the most current mailing and Internet addresses and telephone numbers for federal, state, local, and private agencies that will help get your business up and running;

• State population statistics, income and consumption rates, major industry trends, and overall business incentives to give you a better picture of doing business in your state.

• Checklists, sample forms, and a complete sample business plan to assist you with the numerous details of start-up.

Also contains advice on forming and registering your business, developing a powerful marketing and public relations plan, guidelines to writing a smart and functional business plan, tips for gaining control of your finances, and advice on company polices.

Available in paperback!

Paperback $19.95 (ISBN varies from state to state, be sure to specify which state you would like.)

OR TO RECEIVE INFORMATION ABOUT THE SUCCESSFUL BUSINESS LIBRARY

Call, Mail, Email, or Fax Your Order to:
PSI Research, 300 North Valley Drive, Grants Pass, OR 97526 USA
Email: psi2@magick.net   Web site: http://www.psi-research.com
Order Phone in the USA & Canada: (800) 228-2275
Inquiries and International Orders: (541) 479-9464 Fax: (541) 476-1479

Book Title	Paperback	Binder	Quantity	Cost
Business Owner's Guide to Accounting & Bookkeeping	☐	☐		
The Insider's Guide to Small Business Loans	☐	☐		
Top Tax Saving Ideas for Today's Small Business	☐	☐		
SmartStart Your (State) Business *Please specify state:*				
state desired:				

If your purchase is: *Shipping costs within the USA*		
$0 – $25 .... $5.00		**TOTAL**
$25.01 – $50 .... $6.00		**SHIPPING**
$50.01 – $100 .... $7.00		
$100.01 – $175 .... $9.00		**TOTAL ORDER**

If your order exceeds $175, please call to confirm shipping.
International and Canadian Orders please call for a quote on shipping.

SHIPPING INFORMATION: *please give street address*

Name:

Company:

Street Address:

City/State/Zip:

Daytime Phone: *Email Address:*

PAYMENT INFORMATION: *rush service is available, call for details.*

☐ *Check enclosed payable to PSI Research*   ☐ *VISA*   ☐ *MasterCard*   ☐ *AmEx*   ☐ *Discover*

Card Number: *Expires:*

Signature: *Name on Card:*

CALL TO PLACE AN ORDER
— or —
TO RECEIVE A FREE CATALOG **1-800-228-2275**

International Orders (541) 479-9464   *Fax Orders* (541) 476-1479
Web site http://www.psi-research.com   *Email* sales@psi-research.com

PSI Research P.O. Box 3727 Central Point, Oregon 97502 U.S.A.

149633